Creating Culturally
Responsive Classrooms

Creating Culturally
Responsive Classrooms

Barbara J. Shade, Cynthia Kelly, and Mary Oberg

AMERICAN PSYCHOLOGICAL ASSOCIATION | WASHINGTON, DC

First Printing February 1997
Second Printing September 1998
Third Printing November 2001
Fourth Printing July 2003
Fifth Printing February 2004
Sixth Printing September 2004
Seventh Printing February 2005
Eighth Printing September 2005

Published by
American Psychological Association
750 First Street, NE
Washington, DC 20002

Copies may be ordered from
APA Order Department
P.O. Box 92984
Washington, DC 20090-2984

In the UK and Europe, copies may be ordered from
American Psychological Association
3 Henrietta Street
Covent Garden, London
WC2E 8LU England

Typeset in Berkeley and Bell Gothic by University Graphics, Inc., York, PA
Printer: Data Reproductions Corporation, Auburn Hills, MI
Cover Designer: Minker Design, Bethesda, MD
Technical/Production Editor: Edward B. Meidenbauer

Library of Congress Cataloging-in-Publication Data
Shade, Barbara J.
    Creating culturally responsive classrooms / Barbara J. Shade,
Cynthia Kelly, and Mary Oberg
        p.   cm. — (APA psychology in the classroom)
    Includes bibliographical references.
    ISBN 1-55798-407-7 (pbk : alk. paper)
    1.   Multicultural education—United States.   2. Minorities—
education—United States.   3. Educational sociology—United States.
4. Cognitive styles—United States.   5. Education—Social aspects—
United States.   I. Kelly, Cynthia A.   II. Oberg, Mary.
III. Title.   IV. Series.
LC1099.3.S48   1997
370. 117—dc21   96-39392
                                                                            CIP

British Library Cataloguing-in-Publication Data
A CIP record is available from the British Library.

Printed in the United States of America

CONTENTS

PREFACE

Thank you, dear Reader, for joining us on our journey to excellence and equity. It is a path each of us began 20 or more years ago in different parts of the country, in different school districts, and with different children. But it led us to the same conclusions and the same concepts and beliefs about teachers and about children. We have found, as we hope you do, that each idea will inaugurate a period of growth and development that ultimately becomes remarkably satisfying and exhilarating.

This is not a quick journey that you can complete by merely reading this guide and doing the exercises. It is a slow, cautious, reflective, and sometimes personally revealing exploration, but it provides you an opportunity to grow, not only as a professional educator, but also as a human being and citizen dedicated to improving American society.

The philosophy that undergirds this guide is grounded in the following beliefs:

1. Children and all learners come to school with knowledge.

2. Children (all learners) must do their own learning. Teachers are only guides.

3. Children (all learners) must experience knowledge in order to learn it.

4. Learning is not regurgitation of facts but assimilation, incorporation, integration, and internalization of ideas and concepts. Learning results in a change in behavior.

Because of these beliefs, we chose to develop this material in a way that models our philosophy and leads you through the learning process using a different cognitive style than you might ordinarily use. We chose several approaches:

1. We present research findings to demonstrate that there is a basis for the ideas—being culturally responsive is not just a fad, nor can it be dismissed by stating, "that is just good teaching."

2. We provide you opportunities to do some discovery and critical thinking about the issues and the ideas.

3. We provide you with suggestions you can use and adapt in your classroom or instruction.

As you explore these ideas, keep in mind three things which will undoubtedly happen to you as you become totally immersed in the concepts:

1. When you acquire new knowledge, you will begin to see children and their families through different lenses. You will realize the richness of the diversity of perspectives.

2. As you become more expert in these ideas and find that they work, you will want to share them with colleagues. Be careful—they might not be ready. This is a new way of thinking about teaching and learning. You chose to read this guide because you were psychologically and professionally ready to learn about this most important issue. Do not assume that this is true for everyone. However, we do hope that you will find, as we did, someone with whom you can converse and who you can ask questions and who will serve as a support for you and you for them as you begin to acquire and use this new knowledge.

3. This is not a "cookbook." It is a guide that suggests you try certain activities and strategies. Be flexible in conceptualizing how to adapt the ideas and information to your use. Above all, take risks and try them—not all at the same time, but one at a time until you have mastered that strategy and understand what makes it work for you and your students. You will discover—as we did in our separate worlds and affirmed when we came together—that these insights and observations develop into a belief system that produces a synergy between you, your students, and their parents and gives you a professional energy you did not know existed. This guide is your invitation to personal growth.

We appreciate your willingness to begin this exploration and we are particularly appreciative to the editors who asked us to do this; to the peer reviewers—particularly Dr. Carole Gupton and Dr. John Taborn; to the staff of the Anderson Multicultural Lab School and the Afrocentric Educational Academy in Minneapolis, Minnesota, who work with these ideas daily; to Mrs. Xuan Vu, an exceptional graphic artist who helped develop the visual material; to Mrs. Darlene Safransky for her scheduling support; to Dr. Clara New of the University of Wisconsin–Parkside and Mrs. Olivia Garner of the Kenosha Public Schools, who constantly reminded us that teachers must be learners before they can be good teachers.

Barbara J. Shade
Cynthia Kelly
Mary Oberg

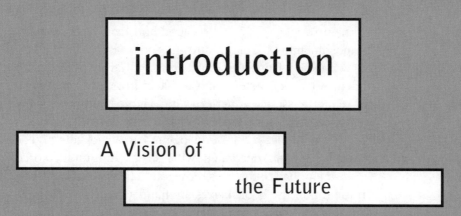

introduction

A Vision of the Future

The purpose of education is to allow a people to systematically guide the reproduction and refinement of the best of themselves.

Wade W. Nobles (1990)

I am sitting here writing my observations and notes for the day to be certain that I have things organized for tomorrow. The children are finishing their work and it is wonderful to see them so engaged. I feel so good and have a sense of accomplishment as I look around the room.

The walls of my classroom are bright and covered with student artwork, posters, and artifacts from African American, Hmong, Native American, and Latino cultures. As my eyes sweep the room, I see student-designed African masks made from papier-mâché and painted in vivid colors. The masks have been decorated with shells and multicolored beads to emphasize the eyes, nose, and cheeks of the figures. On the top of my bookshelves are handcrafted Native American pots that have been created by parents of my students. Wall hangings of elaborately embroidered Hmong cloth that I purchased at our farmers market cover one of my bulletin boards. Brightly colored Mexican American woven straw baskets, miniature crepe paper piñatas, and clay figurines are displayed throughout the room. Shelves are crammed with culture-specific folk tales, legends, and poetry. Student games like Wori, the Stick Game, Pebble Math, Awaree, Go, and Mancala engage students in the history of each others' cultures while reinforcing their critical and creative thinking skills. Posters of cultural role models help students to identify their heritage and expand their visions of career opportunities for their futures. Near the front door a graphic organizer showing an outline of our current unit of study and our daily schedule is posted. I schedule student reflection time at the beginning and end of each day.

The learning areas are defined by walls of individual student storage units and low bookshelves. The classroom layout facilitates cooperative learning, but provides quiet space for individual learning and reflection. Deciding what to put in these learning areas has been a wonderful opportunity for me to reflect on what is important for students to know and be able to do, and the type of thinking required to achieve high, rigorous, academic standards and demonstrate what students have learned. Designing my classroom has enabled me to focus on student academic goals, gain a deeper understanding of students, and gain an appreciation for different ways of learning.

Signs in Spanish, Hmong, Swahili, and Ojibwe languages hang from the ceiling to identify various learning centers and functional objects like doors, chairs, windows, and cabinets. Number systems are also posted in the same languages. Student-, parent-, and teacher-generated expectations for academic success are displayed prominently. The KIVA, a Native American consensus-building process, helped us define themes of interdependence, cooperation, harmony, and individual responsibility while participating as a part of a learning community. It feels good here.

Our current integrated theme of study for this week is ecosystems. Parents and students know that by the end of this unit, students will

❏ understand the elements of an ecosystem and apply the knowledge to our neighborhood communities;

❏ develop investigative skills needed to conduct primary research; and

❏ analyze the interdependence of the biological, economic, social, and cultural characteristics of the communities we represent.

As I look around the room, 12 students are sitting at clustered desks and at one of four computer work stations. I hear students conversing in Spanish, English, and Hmong; their laughter fills my room. Tonya Windfeather, a bilingual Ojibwe-speaking student, and Rafael Ortega, a bilingual Spanish-speaking student, are working at a computer station after researching and comparing artistic graphic patterns from their respective cultures. As part of their mathematics application to understanding ecosystems, the students must recognize similarities among objects and events, generalize patterns and relationships, and use them to describe the physical world, to explain variation, and to make predictions and solve problems. Rafael is speaking to Tonya with animated gestures as he tries to explain the importance of the geometric design of a bird in flight, which is part of his Mexican American cultural heritage. As Tonya is listening, apparently vivid images are forming in her mind and she begins to design an eagle soaring in flight that is part of her Native American heritage. Tonya and Rafael begin to discover the similarities and significance of the Native American and Mexican American symbols through two different ways of expression. They are attempting to portray this relationship as they create a graphic design using the coordinate graphing system on the computer. As my eyes move to another set of students, I see Rahn Jackson, Leonard Olsen, Gaoly Yang, and Racheeda Jones preparing to build a terrarium in the science center. I can detect a mixture of sweet and acidic odors in the air from the moss, dirt, rocks, plants, snails, and chameleons. Rahn is reading directions for building the terrarium while Gaoly and Len are pointing to and collecting the objects mentioned. Racheeda is encouraging Gaoly as she pronounces English words and connects them with the elements in the terrarium. All of a sudden, all four students, in their excitement, shout to their friends to come and look as the chameleon changes colors to adjust to its new environment. As part of the science standards of understanding ecosystems, these students are attempting to replicate the ecosystem located in a park adjacent to our school.

Another 12 students are meeting in small cooperative groups with community members from various cultural organizations like the Urban League, the Hmong Society, the American Indian Cultural Center, the Chamber of Commerce, and the Latino Neighborhood Improvement Foundation who have sent volunteers to my room. Their task is to identify evidence of cultural interdependency within the neighborhood. As part of meeting their language arts standards, students are videotaping interviews with community members representing a variety of languages and cultural perspectives. The interviews center on the issues of how social justice affects individual and group rights. I note that Li addresses Ms. Yang in a respectful manner while actively listening to her response to a probing question.

In another area of the classroom, Jason Lewis, an African American small business owner, is working with students in social studies by developing a survey of the community to find out to what degree community members support their local businesses. As I hear the students engaged in a heated discussion over resources needed to accomplish their project, I see a "teachable moment." I get up, grab a transparency on consensus building, and ask the group to review the process with me for 5 minutes.

In the center of the Reading Area, Marcus Williams is intently engrossed in researching the impact of acid rain on the ecosystem. He is wearing a headset and listening to Native American flute music while reading. I notice that he is tapping his fingers to his own imaginary beat.

This is my classroom and good things are happening here. I know the students are learning because I have seen their work and they do well on tests and other alternative performance measures. But most of all, they seem to want to be here and they want to work and learn. Their actions, their work, and their parents tell me this.

United States society of tomorrow will not resemble our society of the 1980s and early 1990s. The future society will be one in which ethnic diversity will be commonplace. Even today, more than 25% of the people in the United States are African, Hispanic, Asian, or Native American, and immigration continues to change our population, as is illustrated in the headlines shown in Figure 1. In the United States, 14 percent speak a language other than English at home and 20% of the children live in poverty (Usdansky, 1992). The countries of the world are becoming more interdependent, and the use of computers and cyberspace has tripled or even quadrupled. To live in this world, individuals must develop certain skills, traits, and behaviors that assist them to function competently as citizens. Rather than just basic literacy skills, citizens must also be skilled planners and organizers, creative problem solvers, skilled communicators with highly developed interpersonal skills, and good thinkers and self managers with a willingness and ability to learn.

To have classrooms and teachers as just described in every school throughout the country is the goal of parents, communities, superintendents, researchers, and scholars who understand the changes occurring in schools today. The scenario represents what schools must become if America is to remain a country of global leadership. Thus, educators are facing a challenge. As Berliner and Biddle (1995) pointed out, schools are being asked to redefine and restructure themselves to provide education to individuals previously ignored. Now the educational

Our students will need to be:
Skilled planners
Creative problem solvers
Skilled communicators
Skilled interactors
Lifelong learners

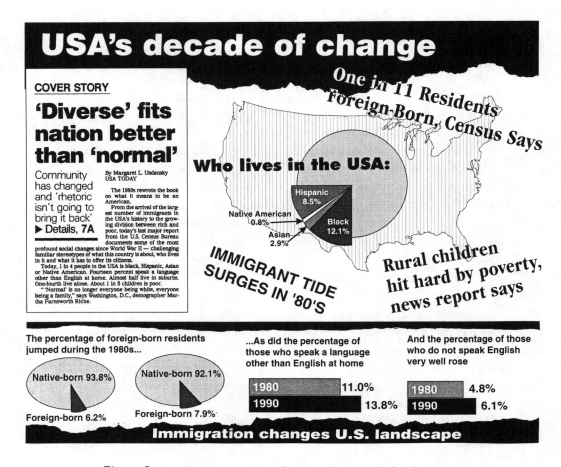

Figure 1. *Used with permission of USA Today, Inc. (Udansky, 1992).*

establishment is being told that they must find ways to increase the achievement of the majority of its clients, not just a few. Children of color, children of poverty, and children of our new immigrants are no longer considered dispensable. They are important human resources that are important for the development of this society. Therefore, instead of the educational enterprise being permitted to address their strategies, curriculum, and approach to approximately 15% of the population, educators are being challenged to ensure that more students—preferably 95 to 100%—are provided the skills, attitudes, and knowledge necessary to become productive citizens.

Why are people in this country so concerned about the fact that there are large numbers of children, specifically those who come from racially different groups, who are not achieving at the level that we believe is appropriate for the citizens of this country? The primary reason is an economic one (Cartwright, 1987). The United States does not have sufficient professionals or skilled workers to help it retain its competitive edge in the world marketplace. Cartwright's observation was confirmed again in *The Wall Street Journal* of September 8, 1995, which reported that although many businesses have many jobs and numerous applicants for those jobs, most of the individuals who apply do not know how to work, do not have the computer skills, do not have the mathematics skills, and do not have the communication or interpersonal skills necessary to do the job (Narisetti, 1995). When one considers the number of individuals who are African American, Hispanic, rural, and poor without adequate incomes and jobs, this seems incongruous. In a country built on supply and demand economics, business has not found a way to keep companies and professions supplied with workers and, ultimately, has not found a way to supply citizens with jobs to meet its needs. Without work, taxes of the few must be spent on public assistance, health care, prisons, and unemployment benefits rather than an infrastructure to keep the physical and social environment of the country in tact. Moreover, Arlene Levinson (1992) and other economists suggest that American society's inability to meet the educational needs of many people of color is depriving the country of a 93-billion-dollar contribution to the gross national product.

The changes necessary to produce educational equity require redefining currently accepted ways of thinking about classrooms and the way teachers structure the teaching–learning process. Such reconceptualizations are rather difficult and somewhat frightening. Now, the curriculum is structured in a linear, additive manner and age-related grades are used. Reformers are suggesting that a spiral, contextualized curriculum and developmental groupings be considered. More important, rather than using standardized paper-and-pencil tasks, the concept of portfolios, performance measures, and other forms of assessment are proclaimed as more appropriate. These reform proposals are predicated on the underlying assumption that children are not robots or mechanical toys that can be expected to function uniformly.

Accomplishing the task of reforming the school to meet the challenges of the new school population begins with the acceptance of the belief typified by the slogan of the National Association of Black School Educators: "All Children Can Learn." Can all children learn? This **All children can learn** is now a commonly quoted phrase, but do you really believe it? If you were really honest and not afraid of being politically incorrect, we believe your answer would be "Yes, but . . . ." When people think of everyone acquiring the same skills in all subjects, they invariably revert to the postulate "All people do not have the ability to learn everything." The concept that the population is divided into ability groups is so ingrained in the American belief system that few people attend to the ideas of Benjamin Bloom (1976) and Jerome

Bruner (1960). These renowned educational theorists state that all students can learn if educators would ensure that the cognitive and affective needs, backgrounds, interests, and behaviors of the students are incorporated into the instructional process.

Is this fair, you ask, to expect teachers to be successful with all learners when students also have parents and various difficulties that are not under the control of educational establishment? If you ascribe to the notion that children from lower socioeconomic status or particular racial groups are inferior, or cannot and generally should not be expected to learn—which is a major deficiency model promoted by many people—then the answer to the question is "No!" However, if you believe that all children deserve the opportunity to develop to their full potential and pursue the American Dream regardless of their background, then the answer is "Yes!—it is fair to expect schools and teachers to provide all students of this generation equal access to knowledge and skills needed to survive in our industrial, technological society." Education has addressed the needs of other groups before, and it is possible to do it again.

UNDERLYING ASSUMPTIONS OF THIS GUIDE

This action guide is not another book on multicultural education, although the results should lead you to engage in multicultural teaching and the use of multicultural curricula. This action guide is about understanding individual differences from an environmental and contextual perspective and will hopefully lead you to an understanding of how better to engage students in the learning process so they can increase their academic performance. Students do not exist in a vacuum outside of the classroom. They touch, they feel, they observe, they think, they act and react, and, as they do, they learn. Teaching and learning are human tasks involving human beings with their own unique needs, understandings, and goals and objectives. To really find ways to improve academic achievement and to promote success for all students require that educators perceive people—our students—as individuals. These students have ideas about how they must behave, they have developed concepts that help them organize the world, and they have a filter through which they see the world. Children, like all human beings, are unique individuals.

Differences between children who are students in our classrooms emanate from more than differential performance on intelligence or achievement tests. Children grow differently. Even though they are the same age, they are not the same size or height and do not have the same physical appearance. Neither are they the same in temperaments and personalities. Although they may come from the same family, they react differently to various situations and exhibit different emotions. Some are more placid and shy, some are more assertive in their interactions, some have an anxiety about how they will function. The profile of emotional reactions varies along a continuum of traits.

In addition to these differences, there are variances that develop because children are a part of different cultural groups. These cultural groups, as well as the families of the children, expose children to the aspects of the environment they perceive as important and teach them different ways of functioning and behaving as a way of survival. The community and the family help children acquire knowledge and guide them in their interpretation of ideas, concepts, people, and events.

If Gardner (1983) is correct, students also exhibit different types of intelligences. Some develop the logical–mathematical intelligence that is highly compatible with the way in which teaching strategies, materials, and tasks are used in schools. Others develop musical intelligence, and some are highly skilled in linguistic creation or performance, whereas many are adept in the use of their body–kinesthetic orientation. There are individuals who are very skilled in handling spatial information and others who develop particular skill for understanding intrapersonal and interpersonal relationships and interactions. Frederiksen, Carlson, and Ward (1984) suggested that these individuals have a high degree of social intelligence—an important cognitive dimension. Because of these differences, educators cannot treat all children the same. This action guide is designed to stimulate your thinking about ways to meet the challenge of teaching to individual differences with a particular emphasis on the variation that occurs because of a student's cultural background.

> Children are of various colors, talents, interests, beliefs, and cultures.

The students on which this action guide will focus will be those who are identified as African American, American Indian, Mexican American, and Hmong. These are particular subgroups within larger groups. We are not examining African Americans who come from Jamaica, Bahamas, or Cuba, or are recent immigrants from Africa. Neither are we looking at other Latino populations such as those from Puerto Rico, Cuba, and Central America, nor other Asian Americans such as the Filipinos, Chinese, and Japanese. Each of these populations exists in their own context and their own environment and learns to adapt and to learn on the basis of their own culture. Although we do not focus on all groups, you will find that the skills of observation, interaction, and instruction acquired through this study material will increase your ability to respond to all students.

The differential examination of the groups in this guide is the result of several factors. First, the groups included are those for which a sizable amount of literature is available, although it is recognized that the information about all groups is multiplying at a rather significant rate. The second reason is familiarity. Depicting the ideas and culture of a group from a realistic perspective and not providing a stereotypic picture requires that individuals have a working knowledge of that community. We selected the groups with which we are best acquainted. A third reason for our group-specific approach is the desire to help teachers find ways to work with students who seem to suffer the most psychological alienation and attendant poor academic performance.

Because we want to show how people adapt to their world and develop particular ways of perceiving, thinking and acting to meet the demands of their environment, we use the social–psychological context in which cultural groups are operating in this society, which Ogbu (1992) suggested emanates from the groups' immigration status. The ecological perspective that sets the stage for the cultural orientations is examined using three categories: (a) *involuntary immigrant status* (b) *voluntary immigrant status* and (c) the *invaded or conquered people status*.

The African American population is viewed as an example of the adaptation to involuntary immigration. This group could be conceived as a new ethnic group as it has incorporated Indian, European, Mexican, and many other ethnic groups in its biological makeup because of interracial mating. Also, this is the group that has developed its own culture, including language, music, rituals, foods, and holidays, and for whom the boundaries of the United States are their only homeland. As Berliner and Biddle (1995) pointed out, whereas all of the groups mentioned are subjected to types of discrimination and prejudice, no group seems to have suffered more than African Americans. As Reynolds Farley (Usdansky, 1992) of the University of Michigan pointed out, "many whites look upon educated Latinos and Asians as pretty much like themselves. Blacks continue to be seen in a more negative light." African Americans, regardless of their class or education, remain the group most ravaged by the rumor of inferiority.

American Indians and Mexican Americans have been assigned to the invaded or conquered category. American Indians were already residents of the Americas—not only North America but also in the land now defined as Mexico and Central and South America. As the result of the invasion of the Europeans, they essentially were forced into an immigrant class through removal, annihilation, and efforts at assimilation. Although it is true that American Indians have come close to extinction, they are residents in their homeland. Their particular educational concerns focus on finding ways to maintain their culture and self-identity.

Using Mexican Americans to represent the Latino population in this country is a decision based on numerical majority. The population from America's neighbor to the south represents over 60% of the Latino American population in this country. Mexican Americans have a history similar to American Indians in that they occupied a portion of Mexico that was ceded to the United

States through the Treaty of Guadalupe Hidalgo in 1848. Suddenly, an entire group of people moved from being a majority in their own land to being a minority in a different land. This community also contains a large number of newcomers, thus giving it a unique status of functioning as both invaded and voluntary immigrants.

The voluntary immigrant group is represented in this guide by the Hmong. The inclusion of the Hmong as a representative of the Asian American perspective provides readers an opportunity to look at a recent voluntary immigrant group who are in the throes of adapting to a new culture and a new society. Of particular interest is the fact that the academic achievement of the Hmong profile does not mirror other Asian American groups.

OUR GOALS

We have established five goals for this guide:

Goal 1: Provide a knowledge base about cultural orientations of the communities from which students come. Students bring certain human characteristics that have been shaped by their socializing group to the classroom, and teachers must be able to recognize these traits and build on them if children are to reach their academic potential. The cultural, social, and historical backgrounds of children have a major impact on how they perceive school and the educational process.

Goal 2: Provide suggestions on promoting culturally attuned motivational strategies. A major concern in teaching and learning is the issues of motivation and self-initiative. Learners need invitations to participate in the educational process, particularly if there is not a history of successful participation. It is the intent of this section to help teachers consider the strengths and perspectives children bring to the classroom so that these can be incorporated in approaches that facilitate ways of restructuring the environment and social interactions in the classroom that motivate students and lead to the development of an achieving learning community.

Goal 3: Examine the impact of culture on ways of learning. Culture has a major impact on how students acquire knowledge because it influences the way individuals focus on and process information. The issue of teaching to different learning styles is an important concept that deserves the attention of teachers who wish to be effective teachers in a setting with students of color; however, learning style is not just about setting up the classroom and using the correct modalities. Teachers also must find appropriate ways to help students access information—or, to use a computer term, to insure they input the data in ways that will allow children to demonstrate the appropriate output.

Goal 4: Provide suggestions on ways to structure culturally responsive class-

rooms. Although many types of diversity exist within the classroom, the assumption of this guide is that if teachers can meet the challenge of creating a successful experience for particular ethnocultural groups, they will develop the type-conscious awareness and pedagogical skills that can greatly enhance the learning of all students in their classrooms. If teachers help students learn in ways that are familiar and preferred by them, they can produce classrooms in which harmony and achievement exist.

Goal 5: Provide examples of the theory and ideas in practice that the reader can translate to the classroom. None of these ideas make sense if educators cannot use them. The final chapter details how master teachers have conceptualized ways of teaching to culturally specific cognitive styles and introduces you to culturally oriented teaching strategies.

This guide is designed to be used primarily as a school staff-development project or as an independent study project. It can also be helpful as a text in a graduate or undergraduate teacher-education course. We encourage teams of teachers to proceed through this guide together because it is important that there is an opportunity for self-reflection and group discussion. The suggested activities to be done are labeled either "Stop and Reflect" or "Action Steps." You are encouraged to photocopy the pages rather than writing in the booklet.

An important aspect of the learning process built into this guide is the use of a reflective journal. The development of a classroom that meets the psychological and social needs of all of the students with whom you are engaged is an affective as well as a cognitive process. To get to that point means you must engage in a developmental process (a journey) that should result in significant change. The creative, reflective journal is an important part of that process. Please use it.

EXHIBIT 1 | **Self-Audit of Your Culturally Compatible Classroom**

You have just read a scenario of a classroom designed to foster cognitive engagement and equal opportunity to learn because the classroom included basic elements of being responsive to culturally different students. Before you explore the theoretical underpinnings behind the development of this approach to teaching and learning, please assess yourself to determine where you are in your developmental stage. Please rate yourself on each of the following elements using a scale of 1–5 with 5 being *making corrections/culturally responsive*, 3 *is starting to put into practice*, and 1 being *seeking understanding*.

ENVIRONMENTAL STYLE:

1. Are your visuals representative of all cultural groups?

□   □   □
1   3   5

2. Do you have learning centers that capitalize and focus on the different modalities/intelligences?

□   □   □
1   3   5

3. Do you establish a routine and daily schedule, to provide some important structure?

□   □   □
1   3   5

4. Do you encourage interpersonal interactions and a sense of family and community?

□   □   □
1   3   5

5. How would you rate your understanding and knowledge of the cultural ways of thinking, acting, and believing of the following groups?
(1 = *low*; 3 = *average*; 5 = *high*):

□   □   □
1   3   5

African Americans
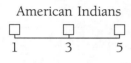
1   3   5

Hmong Americans
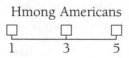
1   3   5

American Indians
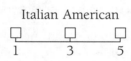
1   3   5

Italian American
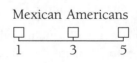
1   3   5

German Americans
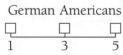
1   3   5

Mexican Americans
□   □   □
1   3   5

Hispanic/Latino Americans
□   □   □
1   3   5

INTERACTIONAL STYLE:
For the rest of the exhibit use this scale: 1 = *never*;
3 = *sometimes*; 5 = *always*.

1. When you use cooperative groups, are you certain everyone understands their role in the performance of the task?

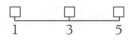
1   3   5

2. Are you prone to heterogeneously group by race, gender, and ability unless the task specifically demands another type of grouping?

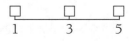
1   3   5

EXHIBIT 1 | (CONT'D)

3. Do you find ways to engage all students in each lesson? | 1   3   5

4. Do you encourage formality with role definitions and appropriate etiquette? | 1   3   5

5. Do you allow students to help each other or to work together even when reading text? | 1   3   5

INSTRUCTIONAL STRATEGIES FOR COGNITIVE STYLE:

1. When giving an assignment, do you provide a global view of the task as well as a step-by-step plan for what groups or individuals are to accomplish? | 1   3   5

2. Do you operate in the classroom as a guide and facilitator rather than a "performer" in front of an audience? | 1   3   5

3. Does *engagement* mean more to you than asking and responding to questions or worksheets? | 1   3   5

4. Do you model and schedule opportunities to practice the ideas or concepts before you require students to demonstrate or test their understanding? | 1   3   5

5. If you use lectures to convey information, do you limit your presentation to 5–10 minutes and have visuals and examples as models of the concept about which you are speaking? | 1   3   5

6. Do you plan ways of helping students process and internalize the information that has been presented? | 1   3   5

7. When you use films, videos, guest speakers, or lengthy readings, do you design ways to assist students to think about and understand the information? | 1   3   5

INSTRUCTIONAL DESIGN FOR COGNITIVE STYLE RESPONSIVENESS:

1. Do you have each day/lesson carefully planned? | 1   3   5

2. Do you plan a lesson or unit with specific activities, themes, or concepts that include material or information to demonstrate connections across disciplines? | 1   3   5

3. Do you use the knowledge of fine arts (art, music, literature) as other ways in which students can gain knowledge about concepts or ideas?

□	□	□
1	3	5

ASSESSMENT STYLE:

1. Do you include both qualitative and quantitative data in your assessment of individuals? Your class? Yourself as a teacher?

□	□	□
1	3	5

2. Have you analyzed the tests given you or the school district to ensure that the questions have an assumption of knowledge with which students are familiar or of which they will become familiar through your instruction?

□	□	□
1	3	5

SUGGESTED READINGS

Cetron, M. (with Soriano, B., & Gayle, M.) (1985). *Schools of the future: How American business and education can cooperate to save our schools*. New York: McGraw-Hill.

Kozol, J. (1985). *Illiterate America*. New York: Plume/Penguin Books.

Levy, G. (1990). *The ghetto school*. Indianapolis, IN: Bobbs-Merrill. (Original work published in 1970)

MacLeod, J. (1987). *Ain't no makin' it: Leveled aspirations in a low-income neighborhood*. Boulder, CO: Westview Press.

Maeroff, G. I. (1982). *Don't blame the kids: The trouble with America's public schools*. New York: McGraw-Hill.

Schlecty, P. C. (1990). *Schools for the 21st Century*. San Francisco: Jossey-Bass.

goal 1

Understanding Cultural Backgrounds

This section provides you with information about the cultural orientations of the groups on which we are focusing. With this knowledge, you should develop a better understanding of how behavior might vary and how the student–teacher interaction might be influenced because of miscommunication and misinterpretation of words and actions. The goal of this section is to explore the diverse cultural orientations of African Americans, American Indians, Mexican Americans, and Asian Americans. Developing an appreciation of these differences will result in a better understanding of student behaviors, student–teacher interactions, and particular communication challenges in the classroom.

CULTURE: THE BACKDROP FOR LEARNING

> We are beginning to realize that a lot of these things which are supposed to be universal are actually culturally specific and without pathological consequences if they deviate from contemporary American norms.
>
> Robert A. LeVine (1991)

Benjamin Bloom (1976) believes that students approach each learning task with his or her own particular history of development and learning. In other words, students bring their own point of view about ideas, the world, and the learning task to the learning process. Bloom refers to these characteristics as the students' *affective and cognitive entry behaviors*. Another term that describes these learner characteristics is *Weltanschauung* ("worldview") or *culture*.

What is Culture?

Culture is a social system that represents an accumulation of beliefs, attitudes, habits, values, and practices that serve as a filter through which a group of people view and respond to the world in which they live. Nobles (1990) suggested that it represents the rules and frames of reference that provide a group, and the individuals within that group, a design for living. Edward Hall (1989), one of foremost authorities on the subject of culture, suggested that culture is a set of invisible patterns that become normal ways of acting, feeling and being. Maehr (1974) defines culture as a group's preferred way of perceiving, judging, and organizing the things they encounter in their daily lives. Thus, culture represents a collective consciousness or a group state of mind. If people in a group share situations and problems, share the same geographical space, belong to the same tribe or clan, are of the same ethnicity or religion, or participate in the same social system or institution, they develop a common way of speaking, acting, thinking, and believing. As the behavior is institutionalized through intergenerational transmission, it becomes culture. Not only does culture provide behavioral and cognitive guidelines for functioning, it provides a sense of belonging and a special bond or unity that every human being needs.

Children coming to our classroom are members of different cultures. This implies that students do not arrive in the classroom as "blank slates." They enter as persons with language, with thoughts about how the world is working, and with ideas about how to behave. In addition, they have developed their own unique ways of thinking and learning. Etta Hollins (1996) stated it very succinctly: children are *learners in progress*. Therefore, the teacher of culturally diverse students becomes a cultural liaison and has the responsibility for developing a connection between the culture of the students and the culture of the school. To accomplish this successfully means that teachers must recognize the various tenets of children's cultural orientation so that they can develop a communication bridge that provides students an equal opportunity to learn and grow into a bicultural citizen.

Using culture as a way of interpreting children's behavior and learning style is not an approach to which teachers are accustomed. Up to this point, the students are judged by the cultural norms of the school or the teacher and are expected to learn in the same way. Any variation is considered inappropriate or deficient. This is a typical response for people who are not acquainted with other ways of functioning or who see the world only from their perspective. Here is an example of what we mean.

An anthropologist published a case study about a group of people under study that Horace Miner (1956) calls the Nacirema. Do you recognize this culture?

> The magical beliefs and practices of the Nacirema present such unusual aspects that it seems desirable to describe them as an example of the extremes to which human behavior can go. Professor Linton first brought the ritual of the Nacirema to the attention of anthropologists twenty years ago, but the culture of this people is still very poorly understood. They are a North American group living in the territory between the Canadian Cree, the Yaqui and Tarahumare of Mexico, and the Carib and Arawak of the Antilles. Little is known of their origin, although tradition states that they come from the east. According to Nacirema mythology, their nation was originated by a culture hero, Notgnihsaw, who is otherwise known for two great feats of strength—the throwing of a piece of wampum across the river Pa-To-Mac and the chopping down of a cherry tree in which the Spirit of Truth resided.

Nacirema culture is characterized by a highly developed market economy which has evolved in a rich natural habitat. While much of the people's time is devoted to economic pursuits, a large part of these labors and a considerable portion of the day are spent in ritual activity. The focus of this activity is the human body, the appearance and health of which loom as a dominant concern in the ethos of the people. . . .

The fundamental belief underlying the whole system appears to be that the human body is ugly and that its natural tendency is to debility and disease . . . which must be averted through the use of ritual and ceremony. Every household has one or more shrines devoted to this purpose . . . while each family has at least one such shrine, the rituals associated with it are not family ceremonies but are private and secret.

The focal point of the shrine is a box or chest which is built into the wall. In this chest are kept the many charms and magical potions without which no native believes he could live. These preparations are secured from a variety of specialized practitioners. . . . In the hierarchy of magical practitioners . . . are specialists whose designation is best translated "holy-mouth-men." The Nacirema have an almost pathological horror of and fascination with the mouth, the condition of which is believed to have a supernatural influence on all social relationships. Were it not for the rituals of the mouth, they believe that their teeth would fall out, their gums bleed, their jaws shrink, their friends desert them, and their lovers reject them. They also believe that a strong relationship exists between oral and moral characteristics. For example, there is a ritual ablution of the mouth for children which is supposed to improve their moral fiber.

The daily body ritual performed by everyone includes a mouth-rite. Despite the fact that these people are so punctilious about the care of the mouth, this rite involves a practice which strikes the uninitiated stranger as revolting. It was reported to me that the ritual consists of inserting a small bundle of hog hairs into the mouth, along with certain magical powders then moving the bundle in a highly formalized series of gestures. . . . (Miner, 1956)[1]

[1]Reprinted by permission of the American Anthropological Association (June 1956) from *American Anthropologist 58* (p. 3). Not for sale or further reproduction.

The culture and the cultural task represented in this excerpt from "Body Ritual Among the Nacirema," has now been identified as Americans who have a ritual related to brushing their teeth. This vignette demonstrates how common behaviors and values of one group look from "the outside." Undoubtedly, the behaviors and cognitive approaches to ideas exhibited by many of our students seem unfamiliar and incomprehensible to teachers because they are different—not deficient—just different than the defined norm.

Before we proceed to identify cultural orientations of various ethnocultural groups, it is important to address the question that is undoubtedly surfacing right now—that is, are defining behaviors using a specific racial group stereotyping? The answer is, "No." Another way of considering the issue is to view these cultural profiles as a *modal personality*—a concept found in psychological anthropology. Modal personality comes from a statistical concept that simply means "most frequent." When we speak of the modal personality or style of a group, we are referring to traits that are most likely to be found in a sample of the population. As Bock (1988) pointed out, designating a modal characteristic does not imply or assume that all or even most of the members of a particular culture share the same trait. Nor does this negate the idea that there are individual difference within the group. What we are describing are stylistic patterns that seem

> Use cultural specific traits as guidelines for observation and understanding children—not as labels.

to be observed in a large percentage of the population. The purpose of illuminating these observations is the same as defining developmental stages and profiles for children. It provides educators a format for observation and for thinking about children from a different perspective. These observations have been made by many scholars, particularly those within the particular communities, and have been affirmed by individuals whose norms, values, and behaviors we are describing. However, before we give you our ideas, gather some information which might help you understand what is being described.

AFRICAN AMERICAN CULTURAL STYLE

The culture of African Americans is an amalgamation of their African origins and the assimilation of various Anglo-European orientations to which they were exposed as involuntary immigrants. The cultural patterns developed are those that not only maintain their ethnic identity, but also help them live in a color-coded and economically disadvantaged environment. Because discrimination and poverty have not been eliminated and because of the continued geographical concentrations of the group, the culture has a strong intergenerational transmission.

Choose two of your African American students and indicate your observations of them on the following dimensions:

1. Do they move closer to you than other students when interacting with you?

2. When with other African American students, do they like to touch each other?

3. On the playground, observe them standing and speaking with each other. Are they facing each other when in general friendly conversation or standing at an oblique angle?

4. When you are chastising them, do they look you in the eye or do they look down or off in the distance?

5. Do they like to work alone or do they prefer to work with others on projects or homework?

6. To what type of information do they respond best? Print? Oral? Role playing? Projects? Pictures? Videos? Computer or building models?

7. Are they expressive in their speech? In their dress?

Now go back and assess yourself on these dimensions.

Are you and the students alike or different in these cultural dimensions?

Are you and your students of the same or different cultural background?

Cultural Dimensions

The most common cultural style dimensions that seem to have the greatest impact on student–teacher or student–school interaction are communication style, personality or response style, linguistic styles, and social interaction styles. As non-Black teachers pay closer attention to the African American community, here are some behaviors that might be observed.

Communication Style

Communication represents the process by which a sender transmits a message to a receiver. Within this process, there is a verbal code, a nonverbal code, and a set of guidelines to assist individuals to use the codes appropriately. Children come to understand that if they are to function in their families, their peer group, and their community, they must communicate effectively. As community members, they are taught an accepted vocabulary, guidelines about what information is important, the appropriate way to listen, methods of getting attention, what represents an acceptable tone and voice level, and how to read kinetic codes.

African Americans have an expressive or verbal presentation style that is uniquely theirs. Pasteur and Toldson (1982) call it "frankness of manner." With tones, looks, gestures, signals, and body language, African American children and adults engage in "telling the truth" or "telling it like it is." Other cultures, particularly Anglo-European cultures in which one is to avoid insults and, hurting people's feelings or where there is a preference for indirect communication or concealing the ulterior motive, see African American communication style as confrontational. However, within the community, it signifies, courage, honesty, and an unwillingness to compromise one's integrity. Embedded in the verbal communication is the use of more concrete, non-abstract words that implore action. Thus, one finds words or expressions that specify experiences, images, actions, and use of natural sounds. Another aspect of verbal communication is the use of *back channeling*. When children and adults engage in back channel behaviors, they make short sounds that listeners make to indicate they are listening. This is a version of the *call and response* pattern and occurs with either the making of a sound such as "um-hum" or the nodding of the head that often occurs within the conversation.

Nonverbal communication is also extremely important in this community. Kochman (1981) and Feldman (1985) defined nonverbal communcation as sending or receiving messages through body language. The premise is that if one cannot risk words, then one can "show" the words. In interactions, nonverbal communication can show support or nonsupport and send messages that suggest whether or not the individuals with which they are interacting are warm, accepting, or tolerant, or fearful and rejecting. Body language also impacts communication stance. Although the communication takes place in close proximity, individuals generally are not observed as directly facing each other or making eye contact. Instead, when speaking to a person, the speaker faces the individual while the listener looks in the distance. This pattern reverses when the speaker became the listener.

This ability to read nonverbal cues and affective dimensions is demonstrated by studies that show that African Americans have a greater sensitivity to facial expressions and have a high degree of social sensitivity than other racial groups (Shade, 1982). Howard Gardner (1983) refers to this as *interpersonal intelligence*. This attention to the social cues in the environment is a very important survival technique. If African Americans find themselves in a situation in which they are faced with hostility and nonacceptance (as is often the case), they need to know this immediately. They make this determination through assessing the nonverbal cues of the setting.

Social Interaction Style

African Americans appear to prefer to work in groups rather than as individuals, which suggests a preference for collectivity, unity, and collaboration. This preference probably originates within the strong kinship network that exists within the African American community. The family for many in the community is a multigenerational social network of relatives, friends, and neighbors (Aschenbrenner, 1973; Martin & Martin, 1978; Stack, 1974).

The preference for social distance in the community is another indication of the social interaction style that exists in this community. *Social distance*—the closeness individuals permit—determines the extent to which individuals receive social cues or develop perceptions of individuals. In the examination of preferred social distance within the African American community, researchers have found that in both adult, college age, and students, there appears to be a smaller social space between communicants within the same community than other groups. Willis (1966), Baxter (1970), and other proxemic researchers find that this is indicative of what they call *high involvement* groups.

Response Style

"Who Am I?" is a major question African Americans ask and attempt to answer in their own unique way when it comes to clothing, body movement, hair styles, aesthetics, and other avenues of self-expression. Pasteur and Toldson (1982) see this as struggle toward optimal mental health by possessing the courage to display style and willingness to gamble one's image on how others see you. Probably more important, this self-expression makes a statement about the lack of invisibility that is often noted by African Americans when functioning in a non-Black environment. It also serves as a statement against conformity that many African Americans equate with slavery and oppression. This individual expressiveness and emotionality are exhibited in presentation style, in laughter, in tone of voice, in level and intensity of verbal and nonverbal expressions, and in music and dance.

Linguistic Styles

The language patterns within the African American community have been the focus of much discussion particularly around Black English vernacular (BEV). Black English is not poor standard English. It is the community vernacular that changes with each generation and time as a way of communicating within the community while blocking the understanding and the intrusion of others. This same phenomena exist between twins and triplets who seem to develop their own vocabulary and communication style. Many words and usages that are embedded in Black English are remnants from the African languages of the involuntary migrants. Few people remember that the slaves were not formally taught the language of their captors. The vocabulary acquired developed from the slave's observations and interpretations within the framework of their own language. Thus, it is not surprising that dat is used instead of *that* as there are no "th's" in a number of African languages. Vansertima (1971) identified several other features that are characteristics of Black English that evolved from African languages:

1. The absence of gender that might result in the statement "he Black," which might mean either he or she.

2. The lack of distinction between second person singular and second person plural that results in *y'all*. Vansertima also noted no obligatory marker for the plural or the possessive, which causes some individuals speaking this vernacular to leave off the s thus "he work here" or "teacher book" rather than "teacher's book."

3. There is also the peculiarity in the verb system in West African languages that results in a different use of verbs. In the West African languages of the past, the verb was used to display action rather than time; therefore one gets the differential use of *be* and the omission of the *ed* at the end of some words.

Labov (1972) explored these cross-racial differences and the intergenerational transmission of these ideas in more detail in his examination of the sociologistic patterns of the BEV. Although there are those who suggest that there is also a southern regional pattern involved, the evidence suggests that there is a distinct pattern of African survivalism as well as specific linguistic adaptations that must be recognized.

To summarize, in general, anthropologists, sociologists, psychologists, and others have delineated the following characteristics of African American cultural style:

❏ an aesthetic appreciation of bright colors, fashionable clothing, and hairstyles as the need to express their self-identity;

□ a deep respect for spirituality and humanness that is often manifested through religion;

□ a spontaneity and ability for improvisation and rhythmic orientations shown in dance, music, art forms, and verbal and nonverbal communication;

□ a value system that incorporates not only the desire for success, but also group unity, freedom, and equality;

□ socialization experiences that develop a preference for cooperation and supportiveness, which manifests itself in group affiliations; and

□ a highly developed skill to understand and correctly perceive the affective dimensions of people and situations.

Variation in how these characteristics are manifested depends in large measure on whether or not African American children participate in the church or the "streets." As Perkins (1975) pointed out, both of these institutions serve as agents of instruction in addition to the family. Both have their own rituals, music, language, social interaction rules, and curriculum. However, the basic underpinnings of African American culture are still present. These orientations come to school with many children and serve as the filter for interpretation of information, tasks, and behavioral expectations.

STOP AND REFLECT I	Identifying Cultural Styles

Copy the questions from the first part of Stop and Reflect I. This time observe an American Indian child or a Mexican American or Asian child on the same dimensions and ask the same questions.

AMERICAN INDIAN CULTURAL STYLE

Although there are over 400 tribes, each with their own languages, history, folklore, and other traits, there is an underlying worldview about how American Indians are to interact with the world that seems to transcend all tribes and is shared by the majority of the Native people (Little Soldier, 1992; Reyhner, 1992). The worldview focuses on spirituality; harmony with nature, time, space, and with those with whom you live; independence and autonomy of the individual learner.

Cultural Dimensions

Communication Style

Living with nature or living in harmony with people requires that individuals learn to be astute observers. As such, individuals from this community pay close attention to every detail of the situation. They see and watch movement as reflected in gestures, facial expressions, or changes in the physical setting. Even when engaged in conversations, individuals within this community are engaged in long-distance scanning, noticing motions in the environment, and identifying objects and people from afar.

Susan Phillips (1983) found that the communication patterns within the community depend on the use of different sensory channels. Within the particular Native American community she studied, the auditory and visual channels were dominant. However, the channels were not necessarily used simultaneously. Each has different purposes and different settings for which they were appropriate. The auditory channel prevails as a method of transmitting information when individuals are communicating and conveying information in settings such as political meetings. However, in ritualistic situations where there is no new information to be transmitted, the visual channel is most commonly used.

Speakers in Native American cultures usually face each other and avoid fidgeting or changing postural positions. Giving one's undivided attention to the person with whom they are involved is an important social value as is showing politeness. When engaged in conversation, one does not interrupt the speaker and avoids the direct gaze or direct eye contact because it represents a sign of disrespect. More importantly, it is not necessary to talk all of the time in a conversation. Smith (1996) noted that silence in social interactions does not produce discomfort for people in this culture but instead is seen as a virtue and an expectation. Equity in time to speak is also valued so the practice of a "round" conversation, which provides every person in the circle an opportunity to speak without being interrupted, is common. Of particular difficulty for non-Native speakers is the fact that getting to the point of the discussion is not a particularly prized approach in Native American communities. Moreover, individuals do not ask directly for what they want. This is seen as a possible area of conflict if individuals do not wish to respond positively.

> Equal speaking time is extremely important.

Social Interaction Style

American Indians live in tribes, have large clans, and like to have social interactions. They initiate face-to-face interactions on a regular basis. This is consistent with their view that everything and everyone should be interactive and has an interdependent relationship. Collectivism, unity, and togetherness are highly valued. Many observers in the community note that there are very few tasks or activities that are done alone. There are always people about with which to share the work, time, and space.

Response Style

The cultural patterns within the response style dimension are best understood by acknowledging how American Indians respond to time. Locke (1992) suggested that people within this culture do not have a concept of time because they perceive that when you are in harmony with the world and others, you simply "go with the flow." Native Americans are not outwardly excitable in manner or speech. The philosophy "Everything is as it should be" prevails. Thus, what is occurring in the present is more important than what will occur in the future. American Indians have a quiet demeanor and time-bound events are not important to them.

Linguistic Style

Although very little attention has been given to the issue, language within the American Indian community does have some patterns that are not the same as "standard" English. Leap (1992) pointed out that the English used in each community or tribe often has striking parallels to critical features of the community's ancestral or tribal language. Using the study of the Ute reservation language to demonstrate his hypothesis, Leap discerned that past-tense reference, contrasts, tenses of verbal action, and subject–verb agreement may be influenced by tribal language tradition. He concluded that, although there are many people of the community who do not speak the ancestral language, there is probably an Indian English vernacular (IEV) that is present in each of the tribes and is maintained as a community language.

The cultural norms and patterns of this community have succinctly summarized by Johanna Nel and Donald Seckinger (1993), as illustrated in Table 1.

To summarize, the culture trends that are most prevalent in American Indian communities and that are most likely to be exhibited in the classroom include

◻ Harmony with nature rather than control of it.

◻ Sharing rather than saving the basic necessities of life.

◻ Sharing praise and blame with other members of the tribe.

◻ Being "right now" or having a present time orientation rather than having a future time orientation. There is a lack of concern for time schedules.

Table 1	Comparing Native American and Mainstream Communication Styles

Communication Style

Mainstream Values	Native American Values
Speak loudly and quickly	Speak softly and slowly
Address listeners directly, often by name	Avoid eye contact
Interrupt frequently	Interject seldomly
Verbal encouragement	Nonverbal encouragement
Verbal skills highly prized	Nonverbal skills valued
Self-expression and self-disclosure	Privacy

Response Style

Mainstream Values	Native American Values
Competition and aggression	Cooperation and patience
Personal goals important	Group needs important
Plan for future	Present is important
Power over nature	Harmony with nature
Control of others	Control of self
Lay fault on others	Shared responsibility
Values material comfort	Shared possessions
Savings for future	Enough for the present

Note: Adapted from Nel and Seckinger, 1993.

❑ Patience rather than action is considered a virtue.

❑ Natural and "nonscientific" explanations for phenomena are preferred to scientific explanations.

❑ Noncompetitive behavior is to be exhibited rather than aggressive competition.

❑ Identifying and being a part of the group is more important than individual accomplishments.

Bennett (1979) suggests that these cultural characteristics are also found among the Mexican American population that resides primarily in the Southwestern United States. Undoubtedly, these similarities can be traced to their Native American ancestry.

MEXICAN AMERICAN CULTURAL STYLE

The Mexican American community is included in the classification of the invaded for several reasons: (a) they have an American Indian heritage and (b) they were invaded not only by Spain but also by the United States, which resulted in the annexation of approximately one third of Mexico. Citizens were then forced to choose whether to live within the borders of Mexico or the United States.

Mexican Americans represent the fastest growing ethnocultural group in the United States and the largest group within the Latino population. According to the census reports, individuals with Mexican backgrounds currently make up 8% of the people in the United States, with the majority of them residing in California, Arizona, New Mexico, Colorado, Texas, and New York (Trueba, 1988). The culture of this group is a mix of Spanish, Indian, and Anglo-European, and elements of all three are present in their environmental orientation. Although the most important dimensions of their community focus on the religion and the Spanish language, there are several important values that should be pinpointed in order to understand the filter through which the world is perceived.

Cultural Dimensions

Communication Style

Locke (1992) noted that verbal play, which includes the use of jokes and humor similar to the verbal play used by African Americans, is an important part of the Mexican American communication style. This approach not only provides a release of tension, it serves as a way of avoiding verbal disagreements because arguing is considered rude and disrespectful. Diplomacy and tact are valued communication skills.

Social Interaction Style

The enhancement and relationship to the group are an important cultural value. Working together, participating in cooperative or collective efforts and developing interpersonal relations is considered an important value. The strong extended family and clan are representative of this value.

Response Style

Experiencing life to its fullest is probably the best description of the response style dimension. It represents the desire to seek rewards and self satisfaction, and "feel" a great deal of emotional involvement with people, ideas, and events.

Perhaps this is the result of the importance of religion in their community or a correlate of the language and the art that dominates their community. Martinez (1977) suggested that the modal personality traits most often manifested by individuals in this community are a tendency toward orderliness, less aggressive interaction, active internal control, and the need to be with people. Male personality is closely associated with the concepts of power, whereas women are closely associated with traits of love, belonging, and religiosity.

Linguistic Style

Kagan and Zahn (1975) suggested that the culture of Mexican Americans cannot be clearly understood without considering the accompanying language orientation. Spanish is one of the world's great languages, yet it has very low prestige in most parts of the United States. It is the vehicle for socialization and learning within the Mexican American community and it is through this language that the children construct their

> Spanish is one of the world's great languages, yet it has very low prestige in the United States.

perceptions of the world and manipulate and learn abstract concepts and processes.

This community of immigrants is faced with a cultural dilemma. On one hand, members of the group promote the idea of assimilation and acculturation. On the other hand, the community is constantly infused with people who bring the culture of Mexico and many individuals go back and forth across the border so that they have maintained their previous frames of reference. Unlike Asian immigrants, there is not a clear break in the ties with the country of origin. The connection with the language and the values and orientations remain strong.

To summarize, the Mexican American worldview and values encompass the following:

◻ Individuals should identify closely with their community, family, and ethnic group.

◻ Individuals should be very sensitive to the feelings of others.

◻ Status and role definitions within the community and family are clearly defined and should be respected.

◻ Achievement or success is highly dependent on the cooperative efforts of individuals rather than competitive individualism.
   (Rameriz & Castenada, 1974)

These values have important implications for how children of this community behave and work in the classroom.

ASIAN AMERICAN CULTURAL STYLE

The group label *Asian American* is used to refer to Asian or Pacific Islanders, Chinese, Japanese, Koreans, Asian Indians, Vietnamese, and the Hmong. Review of the limited number of studies that suggest that these groups have some cultural commonalities such as

◻ Strong support of and loyalty to the family.

◻ A respect and obedience to the elders.

◻ A strong commitment to fulfill obligations.

◻ Compliance with parental expectations.

◻ Dedication to the work ethic and success.

◻ Maintaining both personal and family honor and status.
   (Smith, Brown, & Foley, 1993)

The Chinese and Japanese are often referred to as "the model minority" because their styles of behaving and learning closely resemble that of Anglo-Europeans. In thinking about these groups, it is important to note that the immigrants who arrive have a particular psychological strength: These individuals have chosen to come to this country voluntarily and are probably the types of individuals with a strong motivation to achieve and take risks. McClelland (1960) called this the *achieving personality*. Also important is that the group brings a frame of reference from their country of origin, they have family ties to another country, and they have memories that provide them with important cultural and psychological roots.

However, recent observers of this group, as well as Mexican Americans, suggest that the second generation of immigrants seems to lose these strengths. This leads to the speculation that perhaps the alienation and reality of ethnic and racial discrimination become major psychological stressors that influence their socialization more than community cultural norms.

The most recent Asian immigrants to come to the United States are the Hmong from Laos. Their entry may not have been as voluntary as the other groups because of the persecution and wars suffered at home. Their cultural background is also somewhat different in that they came from a more isolated rural region and had been able to sustain their own customs with less intervention from other cultures. Every effort possible is being made by this group to maintain their culture in the new society. Thus, the cultural ways of actions and thinking are still evident in (a) the rules by which social interactions are governed, (b) their approach to spirituality and individual expression, and (c) their language.

Cultural Dimensions

Social Interaction Style

The relationships around which the Hmong function is within the confines of their own clan. They have no political hierarchy, no royalty, and no ruling class. The clan is the family, the unit around which relationships are built. Like American Indians, the older members of the tribe (clan) are valued and individuals within the tribe defer to the decisions of these elders about their life choices—be it marriage or other important decisions. There are very defined gender roles within the clan, with male members favored. Maintaining the family is important. Thus early marriage is advocated to ensure the beginning of a new lineage. This clannish influence is in direct contrast to the Anglo-European value of individual freedom.

Response Style

There is a great deal of ritual within the Hmong community around the events that are important in life (e.g., birth, weddings, and funerals). The concept of harmony with nature is an important value, as is ancestral worship. The use of animals in religious sacrifice is a part of their cultural heritage that stems from their orientation toward the world in their country of origin.

Linguistic Style

Timm (1994) pointed out some important linguistic differences between English and Hmong. In Hmong, there is no verb equivalent for *to be*. A more active verb must be used. In addition there is no plural modification of nouns, no possessive case, no objective pronouns, and no adjectival form of numbers. Verbs are not modified for past or future tense but determined by the context such as the day or the week. More important, the language spoken by the Hmong is a tonal language, which means that inflection of tone changes words' meaning. Such differences from English prohibit clear communication and meaningful understanding.

The Hmong children are having academic difficulties similar to other cultural groups on which this guide is focused. There is reason to believe that this difficulty stems from cultural incongruities.

CULTURAL STYLE AND THE SCHOOL

The material that has been presented provides you with an idea of what might be in the minds and the backgrounds of the young people who arrive at school from these various communities. It is not intended to provide a comprehensive view nor is it presented in an effort to get teachers to make individual profiles for groups of students or individuals. Teachers do not have time, energy, or space to do individualized instruction. However, the classroom can be structured to provide cultural validation—that is, a sense that the culture of the children has strengths that can be used in the teaching–learning process; a sense that their actions are not considered inferior; and a sense that the school is willing to reach out and develop a bridge that will permit them to function and perform in school and in the society without denying and ignoring an important part of themselves.

As we consider the development of educational programs for children in these groups, it becomes evident that several important factors must be considered:

1. African Americans have a constant struggle with the rumor of inferiority that has permeated the society as the result of the societal conflict on race. Locke (1992) and others pointed out this is a major unresolved issue in the society. To combat this serious psychological barrier requires a rather consistent emphasis on African American success.

2. For Mexican Americans and recent immigrants like the Hmong, the issue is language. The cultural dimensions and the language are representative of their thought processes, and to change the language is to change the worldview, thought and meaning, and the way information is processed. Making such a change means that the group and the individuals lose their identity and method of functioning, which essentially alienates them from their country and their relatives who are not in the United States. Not only must these children be assisted in the development of a new language with new meanings and concepts, they must be allowed to retain their native language.

3. American Indians and the Hmong want and need the opportunity to maintain their culture, even though it has some conflicting values with mainstream. Unlike the Chinese, Japanese, and even the Vietnamese who seem able to maintain a dual identity and biculturalism with little difficulty, American Indians and Hmong peoples seem unwilling to allow a bicultural existence for their members. Forcing them to adhere to competing values, therefore, adds severe psychological stress, which can only lead to withdrawal or poor men-

tal health and performance. The educational program designed for children of these communities must honor their cultural values.

John Ogbu (1992) makes the point that it is not the culture or the language that makes the difference to groups as they seek to achieve in this society, rather it is their perception of themselves, their life chances, and their power. However, there is little doubt that the culture and language of the students serve as cognitive mediators (bridges) of their perceptions of schools, their social power, and opportunities to fulfill their potential. The next chapter provides you an opportunity to explore ways in which culture influences student motivation.

STOP AND REFLECT II | **Compare the Cultural Dimensions**

The following factors are perceived as cultural dimensions in the schools of this society.
1. Can you plot or note differences for any of the communities?

School Oriented Style   Community Oriented Style

Social Distance: Space bubble for
interaction allows distance.

Authority: The classroom is teacher
centered and teacher directed.

Time: Students are expected to adhere to
exact time. Students think about the
future rather than past or present.

Regulation: The teacher defines and
monitors rules and procedures.

Language: Standard English is required.

Sense of Community: Individuals
compete against each other for rewards.

Competence demonstration: Students demonstrate through paper and pencil tests.

2. Do these disparate styles present a problem for students? If so, how?
3. How are the styles of these different cultural groups similar?

Learn Your Students' Communities

Become an anthropologist. Venture into another culture and walk in the shoes of its members by participating in the following activities:

1 *Find out what social manners are important to the community.* How? Find someone from that community in your workplace, church, or social group and ask. If you do not have access, call the community center that serves the community. There is always someone interested in sharing.

2 *Read magazines and journals that focus on the various communities.*
Examples from the African American Community:

□ *Ebony*

□ *Black Enterprise*

□ *Emerge*

And from the Latino Community:

□ *Hispanic*

Your public library and community centers can help you obtain copies of others. If magazines are not available, do not forget to read community newspapers.

3 *Find art shows and ethnic festivals available for your participation.* View art forms of the community. Observe the music, the family interactions, the dress, the social interaction of members of the community while you are enjoying the festival.

4 *Read folktales that emanate from the respective cultural communities.* Here are some suggestions:

Brown, D. (1993). *Folktales of the Native American*. New York: Henry Holt & Co.

Bruchac, J. (1991). *Native American stories*. Golden, CO: Fulcrum Publishing.

Goss, L., & Barnes, M. E. (1989). *Talk that talk: Anthology of African American storytelling.* New York: Touchstone/Simon & Shuster.

Hamilton, V. (1985). *Black folk tales: The people could fly*. New York: Alfred Knopf.

Livo, N., & Cha, D. (1991). *Folk stories of the Hmong: People of Laos, Thailand and Vietnam*. Englewood, CO: Libraries Unlimited.

West, J. A. (1988). *Mexican American folklore*. Little Rock, AR: August House.

Again, remember you can find others by going through the sections at your local bookstore and at the public library. Folktales tell you much about what is valued within the cultural community.

SUGGESTED READINGS

David, J. (Ed.). (1992). *Growing up Black*. New York: Avon Books.

Galarza, E. (1993). *Barrio boy*. Notre Dame: University of Notre Dame Press.

Gates, H. L. (1994). *Colored people: A memoir*. New York: Vintage Books.

Hall, E. T. (1959). *The silent language*. New York: Anchor Press.

Hong, M. (Ed). (1993). *Growing up Asian American*. New York: Avon Books.

Lopez, T. A. (Ed). (1993). *Growing up Chicana/o*. New York: Avon Books.

Mattison, W., Lo, L., & Scarseth, T. (Eds.) (1994). *Hmong lives: From Laos to LaCrosse*. LaCrosse, WI: The Pump House.

Mintz, S. W., & Price, R. (1992). *The birth of African American culture*. Boston: Beacon Press.

Riley, P. (ed). (1993). *Growing up Native American*. New York: Avon Books.

Rivera, E. (1982). *Family installments: Memories of growing up Hispanic*. New York: Penguin Books.

goal 2

Understanding How Culture
Influences Motivation

The goal of this section is to demonstrate cultural mediation—building bridges between school and the cultural communities. When teachers establish a trusting relationship, a sense of community is developed and students become motivated to achieve.

CREATE A CULTURALLY COMPATIBLE CLASSROOM

> Once we have created winning habits and patterns, we can set our goal in a more balanced manner. This will allow us to make a greater contribution to the world and fulfill our true purpose. We can also be more successful in dealing with interpersonal relationships and helping others achieve their goals . . . and support their growth and development of their own values.
>
> —Don Coyhis, Educational consultant to Minneapolis
> Public Schools

No student comes to school wishing to be a failure. It is not in his or her nature. However, to learn, children have to feel comfortable—as though they belong and that they will have support for trying new things and perhaps failing or succeeding. This is particularly true for students whose skin color becomes a major focus or whose culture or language is different from the teachers and the schools.

Children of low social power and status walk into schools where the culture of power revolves around the following beliefs, practices, ways of knowing and behaving:

☐ Student impulses will be controlled.

☐ Rational thinking must be exhibited over emotionality.

☐ Students must approach their assigned tasks in an autonomous and dispassionate, but persistent manner.

☐ Tasks given need not be connected to personal interest, experience, or children's needs.

☐ Individualistic competition is prized over collective collaboration.

☐ There must be low levels of physical movement and stimulation.

☐ Time is a commodity, therefore rigid time schedules must be maintained.

☐ Individual work is expected, therefore students are discouraged from talking to other students while working on a task.

□ Because tasks are disconnected from children's daily lives, the content of the learning activity is deemphasized.

□ The teaching–learning process is considered serious, therefore gaiety and emotional outbursts are suppressed.

These approaches to the climate of the classroom and the teaching–learning process have become institutionalized and taken for granted as the correct way for classrooms to operate.

Enter children for whom teaching and learning experiences differ from this approach! They perceive that classrooms should include emotionality, social involvement, multiple stimuli, movement, experiential relevance, cooperation, and flexibility. They make an appraisal of the situation to see if they can exist in this environment, and when they notice that their expectations differ from those of the school, they turn to the teacher. They ask: "Can you fix this?"

The Teacher: Key to Success

Teachers are important to the success of students. Hmong and American Indian children equate them with the authority of the elders of their tribes, whereas Mexican and African American children see them as significant others such as their mothers or fathers. Through their actions, teachers send messages to children as to whether or not they are accepted, whether or not they are competent, whether or not they can accomplish the tasks they are given, and whether or not the classroom actually "belongs" to them.

First, teachers set the stage and climate for learning that either facilitates or hampers cognitive engagement. Learning to be competent takes place within the confines of discreet classrooms over which teachers have an inordinate amount of power and control. Regardless of board policies, curriculum guides, contracts, and directives, teachers make decisions about the implementation of the teaching–learning process.

Second, teachers send verbal and nonverbal messages to students to indicate whether or not they are capable of achieving success. These messages establish the psychological climate in which students work. The type of praise, criticism, encouragement, and support given by the teacher transmits the message of what the teacher expects of the individual, how the teacher views the student's ability to perform the tasks, and the extent to which the teacher is prepared to work with the student to help him or her accomplish the work in the classroom.

Third, teachers establish the intellectual climate of the classroom by setting time limits, and selecting appropriate tasks and presentation style to meet the information processing preferences of their students. The competence with which teachers perform the selection and mediate the learning process determines whether or not students have access to the information in ways that facilitate their learning.

Fourth, teachers provide visions and images of the future. Although it is extremely important to motivate students to do the work and to persist so that they complete the tasks, the most important aspect of learning is the involvement of the student with the content and material in ways that it becomes an important part of his cognitive or affective repertoire. This means that students must perceive that the information has meaning for them, that it will fit with their current lifestyle and reality, and that it has potential for helping them in the future. The teacher has the responsibility for helping to make this connection by establishing a culturally responsive learning community.

What is a Learning Community?

To develop a culturally responsive learning community requires that teachers help the inhabitants of that classroom find a way to work collaboratively toward a goal. This goal is using, developing, and constructing knowledge. This requires the practice of five major principles.

Principle I. *A learning community must be inviting.* Purkey and Novak (1984) identify this as invitational education in which students are made to feel at home and as though they are contributing members. An inviting learning community concentrates on establishing a pleasant physical and psychological environment that welcomes students. When students enter the classroom, they become a part of school culture, and how the student will function within this particular environment depends on their comfort level and the extent to which they believe the place satisfies their basic needs.

Their assessment of this unfamiliar environment begins with the physical environment because it sets the stage for the degree and intensity of the social interaction. Probst (1974) pointed out that each time an individual enters a setting, the student assesses it from the perspective of

◻ "Can this place be mine or adjusted to me?"

◻ "Can I produce results here?"

◻ "Can I relate and get along with others who are here?"

If Moos (1979) is correct, students are more likely to answer these questions affirmatively if the environment is moderately arousing, pleasant, is mildly stimulating, and arranged for easy movement. For children of color and families of immigrants, their initial assessment of their acceptance depends on whether or not they perceive pictures, symbols, or other visual representations that remind them of their homes, communities, and values.

An inviting classroom also focuses on the use of color, lighting, sound, and the physical arrangement of space. Businesses have known that these are important dimensions for some time, particularly if developing environments that will facilitate employee productivity (Birren, 1978; Mehrabian, 1976). Classrooms are just as much the workplaces of children as businesses are the workplaces of adults. Therefore, the use of color, space, lights, and sounds are just as important. Whereas there are some cultures such as American Indians that seem to prefer the muted, earth tones, other cultures, for whom sun, warmth, and flora are predominant characteristics in their natural environment, love the bright yellows, pastels, and colors that denote activity and vibrance.

> An inviting classroom uses color, physical arrangement of space, lighting, and sound to attract students to the learning process.

An inviting classroom uses the arrangements of the desks to enhance the interpersonal relationships between the teacher and the student. When engaged in the teaching–learning process, it is important for teachers to interact with students as individuals as well as groups. Researchers, therefore, suggest that it is important to space available desks so that the teacher can have personal contact with each student (Hood-Smith & Leffingwell, 1983). In addition, students must be able to relate in a positive way to each other so that communication occurs not only between the teacher and students in a particular vicinity, but also between student and student. This permits a sense of connection and collaboration. As the authors pointed out in their review of physical space, one student unable to participate in the group can alter the dynamic flow of personalities within the classroom and have an effect on the behavior of students.

Good and Brophy (1977) noted that much more adaptive classroom behavior is likely to occur if teachers and students are in close proximity to each other, because students are more likely to receive the verbal and nonverbal cues they need to increase the demonstration of positive classroom behaviors. In addition, peer tutoring is more likely to occur if seating is arranged so that students can become familiar with each other and have the permission and flexibility to seek and give academic assistance. This approach, of course, changes the rules of the classroom. As Delgado-Gaitan and Trueba (1991) pointed out in their ethnography, Mexican American children often view each other as natural resources to accomplish their tasks and offer assistance to their peers. Teachers who are oriented toward the traditional way of working insist that there is no talking, no copying, and no assistance with work. Changing the seating arrangement and encouraging collaboration helps eliminate cultural conflict for this group.

The physical setting can also become an important learning tool. An entire school in Milwaukee decided to study rain forests. To begin their study, the building was decorated to resemble this environment, with the bottom floor developing their classrooms and hallways to look like the foliage and animals at the ground level, the second floor converted itself to resemble the foliage, birds, and animals that might be found in the middle level of the forest, while the upper floors focused on what it was like to be at the tree tops. Shirley Heck (1978) calls this creating a stage-set design and suggested that every classroom needs to be conceived as a stage and students as actors. This, she suggested, makes learning experiences and situations life related and purposeful, and provides a way to bridge the gap between worlds. Moreover, it stimulates discovery and exploration and helps develop more complex frames of reference for the students. Within the context of the teaching–learning process, it also provides language experiences, imaginative writing, role playing, research, and improvisational activities that improve both cross-cultural communication and academic skills. Heck further noted that this is an approach that helps children learn about other people, sensitizes them to feelings of others, and meets the basic needs of belonging and security because they are involved in the development of an environment that belongs to them. This can be particularly enlightening practice for children who have not traveled; but it also allows new immigrants to recreate environments that resemble their homelands and share this experience with their fellow students.

Sutro and Gross (1984) indicated that the classroom is psychologically inviting if teachers pay attention to how to incorporate the various sensory modes into the classroom. They suggest that classrooms must be visual and should be changed visually throughout the year. Teachers must take advantage of sound; this can be done using music—not just music that the teacher prefers, but music identified by the students or music that reflects the times or genre under discussion in the classroom. Providing students the opportunity to touch, particularly if they are tactile learners, and to allow smell and taste to enter in through foods—either from a historical period or even from a culture—becomes a bonding and inviting experience. Eating together is an important ritual in many communities and the opportunity to share special treats, parties, or dinners with parents, other children, and the teacher can encourage students to become an integral part of the classroom (Ladson-Billings, 1994).

Principle II: *The leader of the learning community must send personally inviting messages.* As Gloria Ladson-Billings (1994) pointed out in her study of teachers who are effective in their invitations to learn with African American students, this does not mean that there is excessive praise, a lack of discipline, or students engaged in trivial tasks just to be entertained. What was evident in her study was that the teachers sent messages of accessibility and dedication through their actions, their faces, their dress, and their persona. Children were able to sense that they were special and important to teachers.

A learning community that is culturally inclusive must be led by a teacher who is warm and supportive. Through the demonstration of his or her attentiveness, the levels of expectations expressed, the encouragements, the attitudes, the evaluations, and the language and nonverbal cues used by the teacher, students acquire their perceptions of themselves as learners and contributors to society. Unfortunately, these inviting messages often are not sent to students of color. Study after study indicates that Anglo-European teachers make a difference between their perceived ideal student, who is usually an Anglo-European, and those who differ in skin color, language, or just behavior in general.

Grossman (1991) did a major review of the differential behavior teachers exhibit toward different groups of children. He found numerous reports that indicated that even though teachers have the exact same information about students except for their ethnic or socioeconomic backgrounds, they attributed higher academic and intellectual potential to Anglo-European students than to African American and Latino students. In a study by Veldman and Worsham (1982), Anglo-European students were more likely to be listed in the "good student" category whereas students of color were more likely to be categorized as rebellious or withdrawn. In comparison with Anglo-European students, African American pupils are more likely to receive negative academic and behavioral feedback than European students, and when teachers do praise them, it is more likely to be qualified (e.g., "Your work is almost good enough . . . ").

Charles Moody (1990) noticed that differential assessment and response occurs even though the students are demonstrating the exact same performance. He observed that in schools when Anglo-European children ask questions, explore, and touch, the teachers see them as gifted and smart; however, when African American children demonstrate this behavior, they are perceived as disrespectful and as having behavioral problems. Grossman (1991) noted that research studies have found that even if the children have been identified as gifted, teachers are more likely to give them less attention, less praise, and more negative responses. Entwisle, Alexander, Pallas, and Cadigan (1988) found that Anglo-European teachers are more likely to give African American children lower marks in school even if their personal achievement, family attainment, test scores, and maturity are exactly the same as their Anglo-European children. Recently, a teacher of a young African American girl was asked why she did not refer the girl for assessment for the gifted program. Her response was that her behavior was so bad that she did not want to reward her by having her sent to the gifted program. At no point did the teacher understand that the young student's constant speaking out to show what she knew, correcting the teacher's errors or talking to friends and looking for other things to do, was an indication of her need for additional intellectual stimulation. The student was being "bad."

Children whose cultural backgrounds differ from the teachers are also more likely to get into trouble if they behave in ways that may be acceptable in their homes or communities. For example, African American students are brought up to be more active, emotionally responsive, and assertive than most middle class Euro-American students and teachers. As a result, African American students are often inappropriately referred to and accepted into special education classes for the behavior disordered and emotionally disturbed, particularly if they are male. Teachers also have difficulty with students and respond differently to students who have accents than those who do not, and Valencia (1991) found that teachers are much more likely to respond positively to Anglo-European children than they are to Mexican American children. Sometimes this difference occurred in subtle ways. In nonbilingual classrooms, teachers have been found to leave out or single out Latino students, sometimes forgetting to call on them even though everyone else in the room has had a chance to read. In some instances they were not even included on teams or groups. If Mexican American students made contact and initiated interactions with teachers as a way of attempting to become more assertive and achieving as other students, their behavior was interpreted as signs of arrogance rather than as appropriate behavior for high achievers (Losey, 1995).

When students act differently than expected by teachers, the educators often underestimate the student's ability to learn (Hilliard, 1989). Moreover, if the students are not as attractive based upon the teacher's cultural standards or do not look like they believe students should look, research indicates that teachers do not perceive the children as having learning ability or potential (Vander Zanden & Pace, 1984). This perception of ability becomes the basis for many teachers' behaviors toward children. In research reported by Hilliard (1989), teachers were found to

❑ demand less of low-expectation than high-expectation students.

❑ give low-expectation students the answer and call on someone else rather than try to improve their response through clues or new questions.

❑ criticize low-expectation students more often than high-expectation students for failure.

□ pay less attention to low-expectation students and interact with them less frequently.

□ seat low-expectation students farther away from the teachers than high-expectation students.

□ accept more low-quality or more incorrect responses from low expectation students.

□ in administering or grading tests or assignments, give high-expectation students rather than the low-expectation students the benefit of the doubt in borderline cases.

Although all teachers are not prejudiced and many will deny that they function in this manner, there is evidence that, consciously or unconsciously, teachers project through procedures, interactions, body language, and classroom management techniques the idea that some children are not worthy of being taught by them. Children perceive these negative messages and internalize them to the point that it affects their evaluation of their work and, most of all, it impacts on the relationship between the student and the teacher. For children from cultures in which the teacher or the elder is revered (Hmong and American Indian), where teachers are considered the most significant adult along with parents in their lives (African American), or where warm personalized relationships are important cultural dimensions and considered just good manners, as in Latino culture, these types of behaviors are rejection and create a sense of not belonging.

When teachers transmit acceptance, children become academically successful. Brophy and Evertson (1976) found that teachers who were the most successful in improving the academic performance of students with a history of social discrimination were those who were warm, patient, and understanding. For these students, the teacher who was liked was more effective than the teacher who was skilled, well organized, and task oriented. Swift and Spivak (1973) compared a number of classrooms in an urban school district with suburban classrooms. They found that even though the groups displayed similar patterns in reasoning ability, creativity, and independence of thought, significant differences could be found on rapport with the teacher, work habits, restlessness, and fear of failure. Students who perceived they could relate to the teacher performed at higher levels.

> Culturally responsive teachers are warm, supportive, personable, patient, understanding, enthusiastic, flexible, and stay on task.

Nancy St. John (1971) reported that teachers most likely to stimulate high achievement in African American children are child oriented and display optimism, understanding, adaptability, and great warmth. Ladson-Billings (1990) noted that teachers who foster success for African American students are those who are flexible, creative, well organized, enthusiastic, firm, consistent, and have high expectations, a high energy level, and a commitment to teaching *all* children.

A good example of how the teacher can influence the success of African American students was reported by Thomas Sowell (1976). He wanted to identify the factors that contributed to the academic excellence of students who had been enrolled in predominantly Black high schools prior to forced integration. In one of the more prominent schools, Booker T. Washington High of Atlanta, the alumni reported that the atmosphere in the school was a blend of support, encouragement, and rigid standards. Of one teacher it was said, "She did not tolerate sloppy work any more than a Marine sergeant tolerates cowards on a battlefield." However, the students reported that this teacher was inspiring rather than oppressive and produced a sense of self-worth and pride of achievement.

Teachers have power! By ignoring a child, judging a student, sending a child to the office for behavior teachers misinterpret as inappropriate, ridiculing their language, or showing their stereotypes or their rejection to physical appearance, they create stress and anxiety that ultimately influence student performance and achievement. Just as you cannot make good decisions when you are under stress, students cannot attend to the task and learn when he or she is angry about a personal slight or insult inflicted upon him/her by a teacher.

STOP AND REFLECT III | Analyze Unconscious Behaviors

Look at your classroom. Select students for the following categories that demonstrate students to which you are attached, students about which you are concerned, students who seem to have become invisible, and those you have lost. We know this is difficult because no teacher wants to believe he or she ignores or is not fair to students, but try it.

Category	Student	Why?
If you could keep one student for another year, whom would you pick?		
If you could devote all of your attention to a student who concerns you a great deal, whom would you pick?		

Category	Student	Why?
If a parent were to drop in unannounced for a conference, whose child would be least prepared to talk about?		
If your class was to be reduced by one child, whom would you be relieved to have removed?		

Did you do the exercise using all Anglo-European children? Do it again, using children of color. In the reflective journal you are keeping as you go through this guide, answer the following questions:

1. What behaviors about this student made you select them for the category?

2. What do you notice about your interactions with the student of color you would want to remove?

3. Have a coworker come in and watch you with that student: How many times did you speak to the person positively? How many times did you include him or her in your discussion?

4. Who is the student of color whose behavior is least attractive to you? Why?

5. How do students in categories three and four respond to you?[2]

[2]This is a very difficult exercise because it is asking you to look at your attitudes toward students to determine if you are unconsciously making judgement about appearance, ethnic or linguistic membership, or making other decisions about students as noted in the research. Enroll in TESA or GEESA to explore this further.

ACTION STEP II

Analyze Cumulative Records

1 Choose the student of color who is least attractive to you and read his or her cumulative folder. Divide the comments that are included in this folder into two categories: behavior and academic.

2 Which category of comments dominates this folder? Is this a male or female student?

3 Choose a student of color who behaves as you wish and read his or her cumulative folder. Divide the comments in this folder into two categories: behavior or academic.

4 Which category of comments dominates this folder? Is this a male or female?

5 Do you notice any of the trends that have been observed in the research? Any reactions?

Principle III: *An inviting classroom has firm, consistent, and loving control.* Managing a classroom in which the children come from homes whose orientation toward social control differs from that of the teacher and the accepted school practices seems to create major problems for teachers. There is a fear that the children will be out of control. What non-Black teachers fail to admit is that they have a "fear" of African American students: their vibrancy, their movement, and most of all—their skin color (Henderson & Washington, 1975; Lein, 1973). Perhaps, the best illustration of this is in the classic book, *Thirty-Six Children* by Herbert Kohl (1988). He observes, upon meeting his sixth grade class for the first time,

> It was shock to see thirty-six black faces before me. No preparation helped. It is one thing to be liberal and talk, another to face something and learn that you're afraid . . . I was afraid that if one child got out of my control, the whole class would quickly follow, and I would be overwhelmed by chaos. It is the fear of all beginning teachers, and many never lose it. Instead they become rigid and brutal—everyone must always work or pretend to work. The pretense is fine so long as the semblance of control is maintained. Thus, one finds the strange phenomena in ghetto schools of classes that seem well disciplined and at work all year long performing on tests as poorly as those that have made the fear and chaos overt. . . . (pp. 13, 30)

Kohl further pointed out that for teachers from a different cultural orientation and perspective, the fear is great "particularly if the children are strangers, that is, if they couldn't possibly be your brothers, sisters, your own children, or nieces and nephews" (p. 30).

Unfortunately, in many urban schools and classes in which large percentage of African American students are found, classroom management skills end up being dehumanizing words, physical punishment, and, too often, dismissal or suspension from the room. The behaviors most often cited by teachers in urban schools when they describe the children are

1. They have low attention spans; they are distractible.

2. They will not complete their tasks on time. They come to school late.

3. They lack organizational skills.

4. They speak without being called on or raising their hands.

5. They lack self-control and are always talking to their neighbors.

At no point do teachers attribute these actions to culturally specific communication style of behaviors or even to the idea that the children might be bored with monotonous inappropriate work or that they, themselves, contribute to the difficulty because they do not understand what is appropriate behavior or discipline for culturally diverse students.

Educators use different types of classroom management techniques with children of color and Anglo-European students. Although very little objective evidence exists relative to Latino students, available information suggests that teachers praise, encourage, accept the ideas of Anglo-European students more often than Latino students. One study reported by Losey (1995) revealed Mexican American children being punished for exhibiting the same type of behavior as Anglo-European children who were not punished but actually rewarded. In classes or schools with Mexican American children, Losey also found that children with more Spanish dominant linguistic patterns received more disapproval than others who were less Spanish dominant in their speaking.

In general, teachers of classes with high percentages of African American youth are more likely to be authoritarian and less likely to use the open classroom, student responsibility approach. Grossman (1991) and others have found that teachers seem to spend more time on the lookout for possible misbehavior by African American students, particularly male students. And when misbehavior is identified, the educators are more likely to use more punishment, including corporal punishment and suspension.

The differential use of discipline creates the most cultural conflict as the social control mechanisms used by teachers of culturally different students are significantly different from those used by the students' parents. African American children soon discover that only their most gross improprieties are reported to the parents. Moreover, they understand that the adults at school seem to function differently than those at home and in their community; therefore, they draw the conclusion that they can act differently. Although there are obviously class differences in the way parents relate to their children in terms of control, observers of the interaction between parents and students within the community suggest that African American children are socialized to expect restraints on their behavior (Hale, 1982; Webster, 1974). Unfortunately, the non-Black teachers to whom black students are assigned in public schools show fear and choose not to make demands on students' behavior, show disdain because they do not understand the behavior, or overreact to behavior because they misinterpret what is being done.

This situation does not have to occur and does not where teachers manage with a humane, authoritative structure that resembles the social control exhibited by the families of the children. Janice Hale believes that greater continuity must exist between how the teacher and the parent respond to African American youth. African American mothers tend to be more firm and physical in their discipline than White mothers although the discipline is generally delivered quickly, firmly, and not with love withdrawal. As Reginald Clark (1983) in his review of the family interaction found that African American parents, particularly those of achieving children, establish a status hierarchy within the home and assign and demand that they have the primary responsibility to guide the child's social and academic development. However, the child also knows that parents often set aside personal wants in favor of meeting children's needs and the children respond to the displays of affection by establishing close psychological attachments with the parents; thus, the child is more likely to accept the legitimacy of the parents' decision making authority.

Unfortunately, the often impersonal, aloof, and task-oriented approach of teachers and the errors teachers make in their verbal and nonverbal behavior in relationships with the children does not permit the development of attachment that can facilitate the type of social control that can enhance classroom organization and structure. This, coupled with the lack of variety in presentation or what Boykin (1982) calls *classroom verve*, results in situations that often create classroom chaos.

Teachers also use inappropriate management skills with groups other than African Americans. Philips (1983) noted that American Indian children are accustomed to being raised by a number of people and to functioning within the peer group. Therefore, these children are less likely to be reprimanded as individuals but as part of a group. However, when an individual is perceived as behaving inappropriately, in keeping with the cultural orientation not to call attention to oneself, the child is taken aside and spoken to privately. If, in public schools, the child is singled out and reprimanded before the group, a significant cultural *faux pas* has been committed that is quite damaging to the ego of the child.

Grossman (1984) did a study in which close to 300 Hispanic people responded to a questionnaire that asked the individuals to disagree on certain statements relating to Latino culture as ways of providing some important guidelines to educators about the culture without doing stereotyping. In the section in which classroom management was discussed, the respondents seemed to agree that several cultural conflicts could arise. First, if educators deprive Latino students of attention or affection in an effort to discipline, this may result in a feeling of rejection and perception of inordinate cruelty as Latino parents are more likely to use physical punishment rather than deprivation of affection for discipline. Second, it was also agreed that Latino parents are more likely to speak politely and indirectly to their children, which suggests that the more direct manner of the Anglo-European teacher is very likely to be perceived as insulting and as a sign of disrespect.

Examining the issue of classroom management for many Asian students is difficult because of the cultural orientation. Asian children, particularly the Hmong, are responding toward the teacher in ways not to call attention to themselves for fear that they will dishonor the family if their actions result in negative discipline. The result is that students from these cultures often become "invisible" and just ignored, which is just as devastating to their performance as being punished or suspended. In a recent interview with a Hmong community member, Ms. Vujonya (1996) pointed out that Hmong parents use lots of verbal communication to discipline their children and trust the children to obey. If the child does not, the rules are reinforced again verbally. As a part of the clan, poor behavior consists of such things as going to have fun with friends instead of helping with the chores at home. To this community, the teacher is always right and is expected to be an authoritarian figure because children are always under the guidance of adults such as clan leaders, elders, and parents. Peer cultural standards are not acceptable norms in this community.

To truly understand how best to relate to children whose socialization may differ from your own requires becoming more aware of the community, the home and observing children in their natural habitat. You may wish to visit ethnic festivals, churches, family-owned restaurants, or other settings in which large numbers of families from the various communities are in attendance. Stop and observe and look at how children are managed and the relationship that is developed between the parent and the child. One final caveat: There are children for whom the parents have no answers just as you will not. It is important to note that these cultural explanations may not fit for all children because there are many things occurring in the environment that might suggest the child is a behavior problem. However, the key is to become adept at discerning the difference: When is a child misbehaving because you have not established the appropriate structure and setting and eliminated cultural dissonance so that the child perceives he or she can "get by," and when do you actually have a "problem child"? Making such distinctions can severely curtail special education referrals.

Principle IV: *An inviting learning community provides students with a sense that they can accomplish the tasks being asked of them. It enhances and fosters good*

On the basis of the information presented on cultural styles within the community, what might be another way of describing the behaviors seen as problems of African American youth in classrooms? How might you restructure your approach to eliminate these behaviors as issues of classroom management?

academic self-concept. The issue of expectations and self-concept are often discussed and teachers use the terms frequently. But what do these concepts mean for children of color particularly if racial, cultural, and linguistic differences are seen as barriers to their acceptance in a school setting and thus barriers to their learning?

In recent years psychologists have arrived at the idea that there are many self-concepts: physical, social, personal, and academic. In looking at children of color, it has been suggested that they understand and have positive visions of themselves in most of the areas with the exception of *academic self-concept*—that is, whether or not they are able to handle the work schools ask of them. Developing this self-concept is difficult because of the media's rather consistent portrayal of failures of groups (particularly African Americans), of failure of the schools, of the inability of Latinos and others to speak English, and the overall impression in the society that schools are not for them and will have no real impact on their lives. Unfortunately, teachers contribute to this lack of belief in their academic efficacy in rather indirect and direct ways. Here are examples:

◻ A teacher says to her class when introducing a concept: "I know this is too hard for you, but . . . ."

◻ To an African American child: "Speak proper English!!!"

◻ A child turns in a paper: "Did you really write this?"

◻ A class composed of students of color does well on the math test: "They must have cheated."

◻ Teachers in the lunch room: "What do you expect, he comes from a single-parent household."

◻ A teacher to a Latino student: "Why do you want to take Geometry? You're not going to college."

☐ The teacher divides the class into groups and puts all of the minorities in one group and assigns them an "easy" book.

What these actions represent is the existence and continual perpetuation of the rumor of inferiority. Academic self-concept or belief that one can function in school is difficult to achieve when the institution and society are constantly bombarding group members with the idea that they are not able to perform. Even more devastating, it has a self-fulfilling prophecy when children are not taught the skills they need in order to perform the tasks, are not provided with the experiences that could provide them the insights and understandings necessary for the foundation for learning, or are not taught in ways that are congruent with their particular approaches to gathering and using knowledge.

Probably the greatest difficulty with academic self-concept is the idea that achievement in school represents the loss of one's ethnic identity and is perceived as "acting White." Betances (1990) reflected on his early years in which teachers encouraged him to forget Spanish and learn English. If this advice is followed, Latinos find is that they have lost part of themselves and are alienated from both their past and their present. Fordham and Ogbu (1986; Fordham, 1988) found that African American children who excelled or were identified as exceptional became "raceless." They were not accepted by the White students and teachers as legitimately smart and they were considered by people in the community as acting inappropriately. Timm (1994) noted that similar conflicts are emerging for the Hmong. Hmong parents are not certain they like the idea that their children are learning new languages in the schools as it makes the children "better" than their elders. It also makes them more rebellious. They want them to do well in society but also wish them to retain their cultural ways. American Indians appear to have resolved this conflict by essentially rejecting acculturation. An inviting and culturally responsive classroom is one that does not force children to make this type of choice. The teacher must allow students to build bridges between their own identity and society in ways that recognizes their role in both cultures.

> Can children of color perform well in school and not lose their cultural and linguistic identities?

Principle V: *An inviting learning community stresses collectivity rather than individualism.* One of the common traits noticed in the cultural styles of all of the groups being discussed is the notation that each prefers and emphasizes the need for collective action rather than stressing individualistic or competitive social interaction. Within the writing of scholars who study the groups one finds such notations as: The family or peer group is more important than the individual; the tribe and elders are more important than the individual;

it is impolite to be singled out or to stand out over your peers. This particular value or cultural norm leads to the development of what Johnson and Johnson (1994) identified as a *sociocentric learning style*: that is, the preference to work with others to achieve the task and learn rather than work alone.

In his work on motivation, Triandis (1990), a distinguished cross-cultural psychologist, observed that the emphasis on individualism versus collectivism is probably the most important cultural difference in social behavior that can be identified. The particular orientation helps determine for children whether they will pursue and value their own individual goals over those of their tribes, family, work groups, and fellow group members, thus working to make their own goals materialize, or if they will place collective goals ahead of their own personal goals.

The value of individualism over collectivism seems to be a major difference between "Eastern"- versus "Western"-oriented countries and societies. However, Bell (1987) noted that about 70% of the population of the world lives in collective cultures. Preference for collectiveness has been found in Chinese, Japanese, Filipinos, Italians, Jews, Greeks, Hispanics, American Indians, Africans, African Americans, Asian Americans, and Latino Americans. Review of several studies found for example that Hispanics in the United States tend to be more collective than non-Hispanics until they become acculturated. Those who remain identified with their cultural group pay more attention to the needs of in-group members, avoid interpersonal competition, and stress family obligations. Similar patterns are found for Asian Americans, and it is this conflicting view that seems to create the most conflict for Hmong parents and the schools. When African Americans object to the middle class behaviors of individuals seeking social mobility, the observation generally made by family or other African Americans is "they forgot where they came from," meaning that they tend to forget they are a part of the African American group and have become too individualistic, too impersonal, too self-reliant, and too self-absorbed.

Understanding this dichotomy is important in building a climate in which students from collective cultures can function and perceive they are a part of the learning community. The cardinal values of collectivists are reciprocity, obligation, duty, tradition, dependence, harmony, and an emphasis on family integrity and interdependence. Individualists appear to seek ownership, seek dominance, be competitive, be aggressive, be creative, and exclude people who are too different from themselves (Hsu, 1983).

Individualism is considered an essential part of the American character as defined by Anglo-European Americans and in the definitions of *self* and *achievement* within our society. This approach is certainly an underlying value in the schools, which seek to prepare the citizens and transmit the cultural information conceived as important for success in this society. It is this orientation that schools promote because the ideas are perceived as important for success in this society. Unfortunately, this approach creates rebels within the immigrant and cultural groups because this personality style is considered a liability in communities that value cooperation, collaboration, and unity. It produces, as W. E. B. DuBois (1970) defined, "two warring souls."

Summary

Creating a culturally responsive classroom requires that teachers create a situation in which individuals can live in both worlds without guilt, anxiety, and isolation. As Betances (1990) pointed out, the challenge is to educate students so they are empowered with skills for going into the world of work and at the same time reject rejection and maintain their pride of heritage of community. The principles for building this learning community are illustrated in Figure 2.

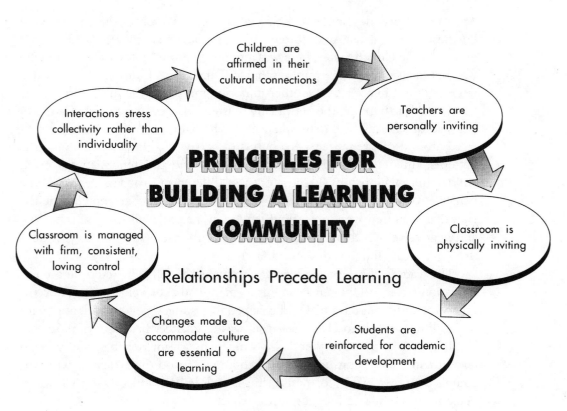

Figure 2

The best example of how a classroom can be restructured to become more humanistic and culturally responsive without losing the focus on the improvement of achievement and acquisition of knowledge is the story of the Kamehameha Early Education Program, now known in the literature as KEEP. The outcome of the work done for Polynesian Hawaiian children, who, like other American children of color, were uncomfortable and nonfunctioning in public schools is important. Tharp (1994) noted that Hawaiian and Navajo people have similarities in conditions known to affect cognitive patterning and socialization. Both are minorities as the result of conquest. By paying close attention to both the culture of the school and incorporating important cultural elements of the children, the school became comfortable for both students and teachers and resulted in increased academic achievement—the goal of building a culturally responsive learning community.

EXAMPLE OF A CULTURALLY RESPONSIVE LEARNING COMMUNITY: KAMEHAMEHA EARLY CHILDHOOD PROGRAM (KEEP)

This project was developed as a part of the examination of the education of Polynesian Hawaiians (Au & Jordan, 1978; Jordan & Tharp, 1979). Like other groups in the United States, here was a minority group in their own land who was not successful in the public schools that had been developed for a different cultural majority. Like other minority groups on the mainland, by the third and fourth grade, the Hawaiian children had become alienated and not engaged in learning or pursuit of success. The cultural conflict observed centered around differences in perceptions of behavior, different sociolinguistic patterns, differences in perceived interaction, and differences in perceived child–adult relationships. Because of these differences, teachers perceived the behavior of the children in negative ways. The researchers noted that the Hawaiian children were gregarious, mutually helpful, talkative, affectionate, and aggressive. Teachers perceived this behavior as rowdy, restless, inattentive, lazy, and uninvolved. (Sound familiar?)

The leaders of the project decided to make the following cultural accommodations to see if differences in engagement and achievement would occur. First, teachers were retrained and coached to assume a new role identity with the children and themselves. The goal was to change their behaviors so that children would perceive them as warm, loving, approachable, and able to teach them many things they needed to know. To do this, teachers were encouraged to give plenty of praise, hugs, and smiles, and to establish interpersonal ties while still setting forth expectations and rules. Concomitantly, the children were given tasks that increased their success experiences in the classroom. The result of both of these actions over time was that it altered the children's habits and orientation toward school.

Second, the classroom interaction was restructured to create patterns of cooperation and mutual collaboration to accomplish tasks. The teachers allowed peer interaction, used group incentives and awards, and used group rather than individual instruction. Children were organized into continuing groups and given self-chosen names. They met with the teacher daily for face-to-face lessons, and teacher-independent desk work was performed in small groups that met in activity centers.

Third, to accommodate the sociolinguistic patterns and the children's perceived cognitive style, reading was taught in a more culturally specific manner. Within the culture of the children, there is a practice for them to meet informally in groups with a sympathetic, warm adult to recreate or recall a story together. To use this approach, the children within the school were organized into small reading groups that allowed approximately five children to sit in a semicircle before the teacher. Although the teacher used a text, the teacher focused the activity by asking questions about the story, speculating about the motives and feelings of the characters, and allowed children to interweave their personal experiences in ways so that it appeared to be a group discussion of the story. The teacher used a whole language approach prevalent in Hawaiian culture: the *talk story*, which is a narrative begun by one student and continued by others who add to it until it is finished.

The changes made resulted in the children becoming engrossed in the schooling process. The result was academic achievement and more academically competent children.

STOP AND REFLECT V | Develop Cultural Relationships

Observe the children in your classroom as was done in KEEP, paying particular attention to behaviors identified in this chapter that may have cultural orientations. Use your observations to list at least two ways you can change your classroom structure or interactions to accommodate these orientations.

SUGGESTED READINGS

Ayers, W. (1993). *To teach: The journey of a teacher*. New York: Teachers College Press.

Collins, M. (1992). *Ordinary children. Extraordinary teachers*. Norfolk, VA: Hampton Roads Publishing Company.

Hale, J. (1994). *Unbank the fire: Visions for the education of African American children*. Baltimore: Johns Hopkins.

Johnson, L. A. (1992). *Dangerous minds*. New York: St. Martins Books.

Kidder, T. (1989). *Among school children*. New York: Avon Books.

Kohl, H. (1988). *Thirty-six children*. New York: Plume/Penguin Books. (Original work published 1967)

Paley, V. G. (1995). *White teacher*. Cambridge, MA: Harvard University Press.

Sachar, E. (1991). *Shut up and let the lady teach*. New York: Poseidon Press.

goal 3

Understanding the Impact
of Culture on Learning

To help students learn, teachers need to appreciate the impact of culture on cognitive and learning styles. This section provides background information about the information processing strategies of African Americans, American Indians, Mexican Americans, and Asian Americans.

CULTURAL WAYS OF LEARNING

> Information alone is not enough for us to achieve the results
> we want in our lives. To achieve more, we must take the new
> information that we have gained and seek to be more aware
> of our own inner feeling, then practice applying the learnings
> repeatedly until we have integrated the new knowledge into
> our life.
>
> —Don Coyhis, Educational consultant to Minneapolis
> Public Schools

What is learning? Learning is a process that leads to some type of action. Through the process of learning, people make changes in our knowledge base and memory storage by accumulating facts; developing and enlarging our concepts and ideas about life; and creating entirely new ideas, attitudes, beliefs, models, images, or patterns.

How Do People Learn?

A number of scholars have developed ideas or theories about how learning takes place. Belenky and her associates (Belenky, Clinchy, Goldberger, & Tarule, 1986) examined a group of women and found that they used several different ways that are also applicable to the general public. One way was the *behavioristic* way of learning—that is, simply performing a task. In this approach to learning, a person in authority makes a demand for action, and the individual does it without having a conscious representation of what is being asked. The "mind" is not seen as operational at all. This might best be described in the Skinnerian model (Good & Brophy, 1977) or the stimulus–response (S → R) model of learning, which means the actor responds to demands. Perhaps the best example of the attempted use of this model can be found in slavery, in which people were asked to perform certain acts and skills without thinking. Another demonstration of the use of this way of learning is found in cult-type religions, which require that people act but not think or reason about their behavior.

A second model of gaining knowledge defined by Belenky and her associates is that of *listening and receiving knowledge*. This is a passive act and relies on peers, family, or other authority figures to tell the individual what to think, what opinion to have, and how to respond. An example of the context in which this style of learning exists might be gangs in which there is a set of rules and a leader who enforces them. This conceptualization of how people should learn also can be found in classrooms in which the teacher merely provides information to students who passively absorb it by listening and taking notes or completing worksheets.

Jerome Bruner (1960) delineated two other models or styles of learning in his classic *Process of Education.* These include the use of inductive and deductive thinking and are defined as analytical learning and intuitive learning. The *analytical learning* approach suggests that individuals know there is knowledge all around for which they must search. Learners can use certain formulas or algorithms to lead them to deduce certain facts, or they can experiment, discover concepts, or acquire knowledge through induction. This approach to learning seems to be most prevalent in the acquisition of mathematics or scientific knowledge and understanding. Bruner's second type of learning has also been explored by Noddings and Shore (1984) and is labeled *intuition.* Individuals who use this approach gain knowledge by developing an insight into or about a situation or idea. Without the usual methods of discovery or proof, learners make a cognitive leap to a conclusion or idea they perceive as self-evident. Sometimes this type of learning is associated with mysticism, spirituality, and subjectivity and is rejected as irrational. However, recent research to understand how people learn lends this approach much more credence. New approaches to the teaching of mathematics involve leading students to arrive at definitions, formulas, or other mathematical principles through intuition so that they have a better understanding of the structure of the subject rather than teaching them to memorize concepts and formulas.

A fifth way of learning is one about which little is written but that is widely promoted by Elliot Eisner (1985). This scholar suggested that individuals and groups learn through aesthetics. As people experience visual images, rhythm, cadence, time, and patterns of the environment, they get a sense of the world around them. The primary method of knowing is through perception—seeing, feeling, touching, experiencing. One might define this as the basis for creativity or doing creative thinking. An additional dimension of this type of learning might be added in the explanation Polanyi (1966) gave of *tacit learning.* Observation is one of the primary ways of learning noted within American Indian communities. Children watch the performance of a task and then do what is required. Because tacit, aesthetic, and intuitive ways of learning are hard to define and to communicate, they are often not perceived, recognized, used, or rewarded in the teaching and learning process.

Most recently, educators and psychologists have defined another category of learning, which they label *constructivist learning.* This type of learning takes place when individuals create their own models, theories, or representations of ideas. They take what they perceive to be important information and integrate it and connect with their own experiences or conceptualization of the world. Individuals who learn in this way develop their own sense of order and construction of reality.

Although individuals may learn best using one or more of these models, they tend to approach the learning process on the basis of their previous experiences, their own personality, and their culture. This is *style* or a set of preferred strategies about thinking that seem to work best for that particular individual.

According to Messick (1994), individuals may be described in terms of one of the following: expressive, response, cognitive, and learning styles. *Expressive styles* include gestures, movements, and facial, vocal, and graphic expression and are likely to be found in our personality traits such as liking variety and action or behavioral verve such as described by Boykin (1994). *Response styles* are reactions to the environment, such as being an extrovert or an introvert and being more oriented toward people and social situations as opposed to tasks and objects; these reactions define our temperament and personality. Our concern in this section is about learning styles and cognitive styles. Although the terms are often used interchangeably, they relate to quite different types of phenomena.

Cognitive Styles and Learning Styles: What Are They?

Learning styles are individually preferred orientations about what factors in our environment seem to facilitate our acquisition of knowledge. These preferences include individual orientation toward social interactions during study time, the types of reward structures that motivate the individual to persist and try harder, and the types of stimulation or noise interference (silence vs. music) that can be tolerated while one is thinking. Differences are found in individual preferences for the types of lighting, temperature, and furniture that assist concentration. For example, Dunn and Dunn (1975) found that individuals develop preferences for the colors that are in the classrooms, the amount of light, and room temperature. Moreover, there are variations in preferred studying postures. Some individuals prefer to sit erect and at a traditional desk, whereas others prefer to stand or recline.

The second dimension of learning style focuses on the extent to which students take responsibility for their own learning. Teachers often assume that the desire to learn is inherently embedded in the student when he or she arrives in the classroom. This is not the case. As with other aspects of learning, the extent to which individuals are engaged depends on their goals, needs, and interests. In addition, the "style" that becomes a part of an individual's personality depends on how students have been socialized to use their environmental resources to achieve certain goals. For example, some are taught to rely on others for assistance, follow the directions as given, and perform the task as modeled. Others are encouraged to be independent and work alone to find their solutions before seeking assistance. Corno and Mandinach (1983) referred to this stylistic dimension as *resource management* and indicated that students select the approach that makes them appear most competent.

Cognitive styles, on the other hand, are the intellectual aspects of learning styles and represent culturally attuned ways of perceiving, organizing, and evaluating information. The strategies preferred by individuals are those used as a part of the internal workings of the mind when processing information. The processes included in cognitive style are perception (cues to which they attend), conceptualization (categorization), and decision making or evaluation (thinking). When students are confronted with information in the school setting, the process probably operates as follows:

□ The teacher presents (book, lecture, media)

□ The student perceives and registers the information

□ The student attaches the idea to some concept or idea already in his or her memory (prior knowledge)

□ The student finds some way to use the information so that it has personal meaning (learning takes place)

The model that represents how we think of the process with culture acting as a filter is presented in Figure 3.

Psychologists have long understood that individuals do not see or think about the same information in the same way. Here is an example of different styles of thinking in operation:

Imagine a teacher who gives her students sets of blocks and asks them to create a building. To help the students, she gives them a set of cards that picture the building from different perspectives: front, back, left, right, and aerial. The complexity of the task is to use two-dimensional pictures to create a three-dimensional building. Some students can view the cards and create the exact replica of the building. Other students need to recreate one view of the building at a time. Other students do not even know where to begin.

Students who can build the building immediately are able to see the big picture and tend to have a more global view of the world. They are the students whose field-dependent cognitive style allows them to see the whole before they see the parts.

Students who need to build the building by using one view at a time usually start with the front view of the building. Then they look at the top view

Information Processing

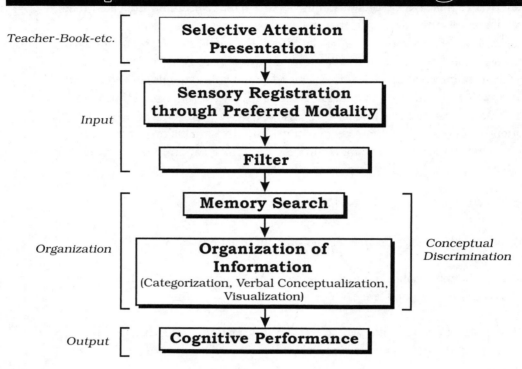

Figure 3

and adjust the blocks to reflect these two views of the building. They proceed to create the building by systematically using the sequence of pictures in order to help them change and readjust the blocks. These students possess a field-independent cognitive style that allows them to see the parts in order to create the whole.

The students who do not know where to start need a set of directions and questions that will aid them in constructing the different separate views of the building so that they match the two-dimensional pictures on each card. The questions also help to guide the students to new observations and discoveries so that they can acquire the knowledge to go on and solve the problem.

Teachers who interact with these students may mistakenly assume that there are differences in ability. However, a more plausible explanation might be that the students have different cognitive or information-processing styles. The example is an excellent illustration of differences in field dependence and field independence.

The dimension of field-dependent and field-independent cognitive styles is the most researched of all cognitive style dimensions and is most often cited when discussing how people process information. Conceptualized and developed by Herman A. Witkin and his associates (Witkin, Moore, Goodenough, & Cox,1977), the concept is perceived to include both perceptual, attentional, and personality characteristics (Witkin et al., 1977). Dembo (1988) delineated the characteristics for each of these styles as follows:

Field-dependent students

□ Perceive globally;

□ Experience information holistically;

□ Make broad general distinctions among concepts;

□ See relationships;

□ Learn material best with social content;

□ Attend best to material relevant to own experience;

□ Require an organizational framework; and

□ Internalize criticism.

Rameriz and Castenada (1974) preferred to use the term *field sensitive* rather than *field dependent* as a way of removing the value judgment from this dimension.

Field-independent individuals are described by Dembo (1988) as those who

□ Perceive analytically and sequentially;

□ Experience information in a segmented fashion;

□ Impose structure or restrictions on information;

□ Learn social material only as an intentional task;

□ Develop interest in new concepts for their own sake;

□ Provide for self-structure for situations; and

□ Ignore or pay little attention to criticism.

As one examines the way in which individuals think or process information, one finds that groups tend to use a particular type of cognitive style as opposed to others because it is congruent with their way of functioning in their society. As Witkin (1978) pointed out, cognitive styles develop to fit the life situations with which the individual or group must cope. This does not mean that styles cannot be changed or that the culturally specific cognitive styles that we identify in the upcoming section cannot be modified to facilitate student learning within the school context. Hilliard (1989) maintained, "Styles are learned, not innate. Like other learned behaviors, styles can be changed." However, rather than seeking to change the cognitive style of students, the teacher should be aware of the style and find a way to develop *cognitive style attunement*, which is a way of ensuring that students maintain their cultural style while acquiring the style important for academic achievement.

CULTURALLY SPECIFIC COGNITIVE STYLES

Psychologists have defined a number of bimodal thinking styles. On one hand, as Hilliard (1976) pointed out, there are those who break down ideas, events, and details into the smallest components and approach information from what might be defined as *objectivity*. Things, tasks, and events are seen as discrete entities that can be processed in a linear, sequential fashion. Words, stories, writing, and mathematics problems are processed through separation or use of a formula. Each idea must follow sequentially. These thinkers are generally perceived as being field independent or analytical or successive processors. On the other hand, there are processors who ignore the detail and concentrate on the relationship of the details to each other (i.e., the whole or the context in which the details are displayed). These are synthesizers and individuals who can bring together divergent ideas and divergent experiences (Willis, 1989). Individuals who process information in this manner are considered to be simultaneous processors (Das, Kirby, & Jarmon, 1975). These types of individuals also are labeled as field-dependent thinkers.

> Cognitive style is an individual's preferred way of processing and organizing information and the environment to fit his or her view of the world.

Inasmuch as culture is the collective consciousness or "personality" of a group, it is not surprising to find that the group develops culturally specific ways of learning and thinking. Unfortunately, the concept of a cultural thinking style is difficult to comprehend because conventional wisdom suggests that all individuals think or reason about ideas in similar fashions. This perception is based on the Anglo-European view of the world. As Hamill (1990) pointed out, individuals who ascribe to this belief consider textbook logic as the norm and analytical thinking as the only way to reason. Proponents of this belief system assume that rationality is better than emotionality, print information has more validity than oral information, abstract conceptualizations are better and more superior to concrete conceptualizations, field independence is better than field dependence, analytical thinking is superior to wholistic thinking, and knowledge acquisition through the intellect is better than learning through intuition (Arnheim, 1985; Goody, 1977; Hallpike, 1979; Hamill, 1990; Stigler & Baranes, 1988). Fortunately, the more education researchers know about learning and learning strategies, the more these value-laden ideas are being challenged. Becoming aware of how different groups have socialized their children to learn provides teachers the opportunity to enhance the potential of students in all areas of functioning.

Culture appears to dictate the style individuals use in their perceptual, attentional, conceptual, and thinking activities. The styles that have been identified for the groups on which we are focusing have emerged generally in the last decade. There is still more information to be gleaned. It is also important to remember that this discussion is not meant to imply that all students of a given group function in a given way. The characteristics of learning styles that have been outlined previously are, however, guidelines for observation and reflection that teachers can use to consider how best to approach students to facilitate their success.

African American Cognitive Style

If one were to define the basic underlying foundation of African American culture, it could be summarized in the word *survival*. The loss of self and identity through slavery, lynchings, and legal segregation was very traumatic for this community, and cultural traits seem oriented toward protecting the psyche and facilitating adaptation to a hostile environment (Pasteur & Toldson, 1982). The style of processing observed in this community seems to verify this hypothesis.

Perceptual Style

In recent years, psychologists have become more aware of the importance of modalities in focusing individual attention on information as they have become more knowledgeable about the way in which individuals receive information in the brain. Sylwester (1995) pointed out that the human sensory organs reach for information beyond the limits of the body to bring input to our neural system and to transform seemingly unconnected and meaningless information into an integrated whole. Psychologists suggest that human beings are taught to perceive, which sets the stage for cognitive development.

Information is gathered by all six sensory channels, but the majority of the information in our society, particularly in schools, is transmitted through visually oriented material. Vision is seen as the "queen" of the sensory registers. However, research suggests that individuals develop a preferential hierarchy for the senses they prefer to use (Barsch, 1971; Shade, 1982).

Barsch examined the development of the use of sensory modes and argued that, whereas people learn to use all of the modes alternately, they develop a prioritized use of the mediation channels depending on which works most efficiently for them in processing information. Experts in the field of neurolinguistic programming (NLP) refer to this as having different representational styles with particular attention to visual, auditory, and kinesthetic representational styles. The visual learner is one who prefers information represented through images such as pictures and photographs and likes to learn by watching and observing. The aural or auditory learner prefers verbal representation of ideas, whereas the kinesthetic learner wishes to hold, touch, and manipulate the material and relies on feelings or affective dimension (Brooks, 1989).

The perceptual styles used in the African American community appear to be multimodal. In his book *Urban Blues*, Charles Keil (1966) noted that certain modes of perception are more characteristic in the African American community than in the European community:

> [I]ts modes of perception and expression, its channels of communication are predominantly auditory and tactile rather than visual and literal. . . . the prominence of the aural perception, oral expression and kinesic codes . . . sharply demarcates the culture from the white world. (pp. 16–17)

Recent research with students suggests that although students like to be have oral presentations and oral interactions, they largely prefer visual (viz., photographs, pictures, or some other form, but not print) and kinesthetic-tactile information (Shade, 1994). Pasteur and Toldson (1982) suggested that African Americans need and use multiple senses to acquire information and perception—bodily movement, the development and projection of images, oral communication of ideas, and the aural development of natural sound.

African American children need kinetic interaction, and this is stated throughout the literature. Morgan (1990) monitored the number of times students initiated some interaction or decided to do something other than the assigned tasks and found that African American children are more likely to be physically and socially active than Anglo-European children. Male African Americans were five times more likely than male Anglo-Europeans to initiate conversation with others, to act out to get attention, or to move around. In another study, Della Valla (1984) found that only 25% of the children could remain seated or passively involved as required by school culture. North (1978) studied the human personality and psyche through movement and found that one can tell a great deal about people by the way they use their body, where the body moves in the surrounding space, and the general style and quality of movement. As any teacher or observer of African American students knows, movement and body style are important aspects of the way in which African Americans express their personalities, whether it is through the tilt of the walk, the decoration in hair and dress, or the rhythm during games or dance.

Attentional Style

An accompanying process of perception is attention. Millions of cues bombard the mind and, unless they are carefully filtered, the brain becomes over-stimulated. Therefore, the cultural community socializes the individuals within that community to attend to certain types of cues. The cues can vary from affective factors representing emotions, spatial cues to help individual orientation to the environment, or object- or material-oriented cues that provide details about things encountered in the physical environment. Studies by Cutrona and Feshbach (1979), Damico (1985), Ruble and Nakamura (1972), and others suggest that African Americans pay more attention to people in their environment than to spatial or object-oriented cues. As a result, they are better able to distinguish emotions, to recognize faces, and to discern certain nuances in social situations than European Americans or other groups with which they have been compared.

A companion trait of this attentional style is the personality style or response style of African Americans, which appears to lean more toward *extroversion* than introversion. Jung (Jung, 1959; Myers, 1980) described extroversion as a preference for perceptual attention directed toward people and their actions and toward arenas of self-expression and as an orientation toward interacting with people and having social relationships. Studies of various African American samples and others suggest that individuals within this culture seek out and attend to people and social situations (Levy, Murphy, & Carlson, 1972; Shade, 1989c). Furthermore, Boykin (1982) indicated that their attention is best focused on tasks if a variety of information is presented at a constantly changing pace.

Conceptual Style

The organization of the massive amount of information that is fed to the mind through the sensory organs requires sorting information into appropriate categories or lumping them in ways that allow the individual to process or handle the information. Again, research studies have found that like other international samples, African Americans use very different categories than European Americans for sorting out information. In addition to different concept differentiation, African Americans have a different perception of the value and meaning of words. Rychlak (1975) suggested from his research that African Americans seem to prefer materials and contexts with affective or more socio-emotional meanings than more impersonal material. Smith and Lewis (1985) found that African American children were more likely to remember and comprehend materials that related to their environmental or cultural orientation.

Inasmuch as knowledge to be acquired is a social as well as a psychological construction of knowledge, it is important for African American children to perceive that taught material has some relationship to their idea of reality. Generally, however, they are asked to acquire and use material and ideas that appear to have little intrinsic or extrinsic value. The material often does not contain elements of their culture, their community, or their political or economic perspectives and often ignores their existence. This omission is being corrected: more attention is being directed toward multicultural textbooks and multicultural orientation and perspectives within the curriculum.

Thinking Style

Research on cognitive processing styles indicates that African Americans are more likely to consider information in a wholistic, relational, and field-dependent manner than are Anglo-Europeans. The studies of this field dependence–independence using African American samples have been done throughout the 1970s and 1980s. Generally, the studies compared different ethnic groups and found that African Americans differed significantly from other groups in their approach to the embedded figures. Even when not compared to other ethnic groups, however, the type of reasoning displayed, on the average, suggested that there were more synthesizers in the group than sequential, detail-oriented processors.

A caveat: It would be very easy to dismiss this finding by suggesting that the Embedded Figures Test is another intelligence test and that this is an ability dimension rather than a reasoning dimension. Cognitive researchers who have examined the performance of different groups in different contexts have concluded that the cognitive tasks once thought to indicate intelligence are really no more than cultural tasks. In a study of the performance of African Americans and American Indians on the test (Shade, 1989c) that measures field orientation, perceptual style and perceptual training were found to have a major impact on the results on this test. Thus, if African Americans attend to social rather than object cues, prefer kinesthetic information, and use figural–pictorial manipulation differently because of socialization, it is very likely that they will be field dependent.

American Indian Cognitive Style

To understand the processing style of Native American children, it is important to become acquainted with their stages of socialization, because this is perceived as an important stage of learning. Although the majority of the research uses the Native American tribes in the Southwest (Navajo, Pueblo) and some Canadian tribes, a review by members of the tribes in Wisconsin suggested that there is great similarity in the response and the learning style used by these community learners (Smith, 1996). Such stages are demonstrated in the Navajo tradition by Smith (1996), who referred to them as *one's development by thoughts* (*Nitsahakees Bee Haho'dilyáa*).

STAGE 1. One Becomes Aware (*Hani Hazlii*). Between the ages of 2 and 4, the individual—now considered a child—is aware of his or her environment and begins to develop his or her own life story. One begins to remember—that is, the brain begins to store experiences as memories.

STAGE 2. One Becomes Self-Aware (*Adaa Akozhniidzii*). Between the ages of 4 and 6, the child learns his or her sex role and begins to imitate the elders. Storytelling is used as an important vehicle to teach the child about Mother Earth and the right and respectful way of relating to nature and all living things.

STAGE 3. One Begins to Think and Do Things (*Nitsidzikees Dzizlii*). Between the ages of 6 and 9, the child begins to practice the lessons learned from the elders. He or she learns to make sacrifices and assume adult responsibility in accordance with his or her gender.

STAGE 4. One's Thought Begins Existing (*Hanitsekees Niliinii Hazlii*). Between the ages of 10 and 15, the individual is expected to remember and demonstrate an accurate understanding of the tribal stories by practicing the principles in daily life. The student is socialized to consider the harmonious relationships of the land, the home, thought, and the sacredness of all. It is also the time for orientation and transformation to adulthood.

STAGE 5. One Begins to Think for Oneself (*Ada Nitzidzikees Dzizlii*). The period of late adolescence (15–18) is the period in which the youth demonstrates independence and full responsibility for individual actions and behavior, an understanding of the cultural principles of the tribe, and the inculcation of these principles into his or her worldview and lifestyle.

STAGE 6. One Begins to Think About All Things (*Taa Attsoni Baanitsidzikees Dzizlii*). During young adulthood (17–22), the individual is perceived to have achieved mastery of the concepts, principles, beliefs, and values of the American Indian and to be ready to begin life independently.

These ideas were extracted from studies of the following tribes: Intuits, Cherokee, Navajo, Pueblo, Papago, Sioux, Warm Springs Oregon, Menomonee, Seminole, and Native Hawaiian. Although there may be some variation in tribes, the basic goals of socialization appear to be the same: growth in independence, harmony with nature and all living things, and mastery of their cultural values and expectations. Observations about the processing styles promoted in this community are presented below.

Perceptual Style

Native American children consistently are found to learn best through the visual sensory modality than through others. They are good at remembering visual symbols, manipulating pictures and designs, and understanding visual relationships. This seems to be true regardless of the tribe involved in the study (Kaulback, 1984). Children are taught to listen (to the stories of the elders), watch (the actions of elders and others), then do what is required. The use of the visual modality is also an important learning mode. Native American children are urged to watch-then-do and to explore and experiment with their environment as a way of learning (More, 1987; Swisher & Deyhle, 1992). Observers note, however, that the verbal–oral mode is used as a secondary modality to call attention to what the children should observe, rather than using it to define the task or idea.

Attentional Style

The ethnographic studies of the communities tend to suggest that Native American children are taught to focus their attention on everything in their environment at the appropriate time. This includes both the people and the physical objects who are in their environment. Researchers report that Native Americans can perceive the slightest movement in gestures and eye expressions and can identify relatives or others from great distances. However, their general personality orientation would probably be toward introversion because they are autonomous, analyze what they perceive, and concentrate their attention on understanding how they fit into the scheme of things. The children are welcomed spectators of family and community events and affairs that inspire their curiosity about all things.

Conceptual Style

Little is known about the preferred categories in Native American culture because very little research seems to have been done. However, one can conclude that the children learn to organize their observations into appropriate categories, which provide them a model for their performance. Categorization generally refers to the linguistic categories used to represent ideas and concepts. Perhaps, as a visual learner, the American Indian child conceptualizes ideas in models, webs, or visual images. The only evidence we have of the conceptualization is the performance, when given, is one that demonstrates competence in the entire task rather than around specific details.

Thinking Style

Using the traditional cognitive style test of field independence and field dependence, Native American children can be considered to be field independent (Dinges & Hollenbeck, 1978; Utley, 1983). This is not surprising in view of their cultural background. The development and production of geometric figures are an important part of the culture, and children are taught to function in a visual–spatial world. These experiences provide Native children the skills to do the Embedded Figures Test with little difficulty (Shade, 1989b, 1989c). At the same time, their ability to observe, manipulate, experiment, and contextualize ideas and information indicates that they are global processors. Tharp (1989) suggested that this type of processing is associated with the observation learning in which the students are consistently engaged, which in turn suggests that these children learn to attend to details but also need to contextualize and approach ideas from a more wholistic perspective. It appears to be an ideal balance of the use of the right and left hemispheres of the brain (More, 1987; Suina & Smolkin, 1994; Swisher & Deyhle, 1992).

American Newcomers and Cognitive Style

The current report issued by the Census Bureau on March 14, 1996, indicates that Hispanics and Asians will account for more than half the growth in the U.S. population every year for the next half century and beyond. They indicate that currently the U.S. population is 12% Black, 10.2% Hispanic, 3.3%

Changing School Population

Projections by the U.S. Bureau of the Census show that by 2030 one in four school-age children will be Hispanic.

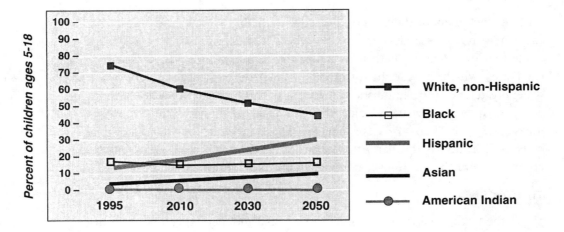

Figure 4. *Note: Percents do not add to 100 because the Hispanic population includes members of several races, including Blacks and Whites. Adapted from U.S. Bureau of the Census March 20, 1996. Education Week XV, No. 26.*

Asian, 73.8% White (not Hispanic), and 0.7% American Indian. By the year 2050, it is forecast that the United States will be 52.8% White, 13.6% Black, 24.5% Hispanic, 8.2% Asian, and 0.9% American Indian (see Figure 4). Despite this potential growth spurt among the Hispanic and Asian communities, however, very little is known about how children coming from these groups learn or how they prefer to process information. Although there are not many studies on the cognitive style of Mexican and Asian Americans, the few existing ones allow for some speculation.

Perceptual Style

Rameriz and Castenada (1974) suggested that Mexican American children tend to be field dependent and that this is traceable to their strong family ties and respect and obedience to elders. They also appear to be more cooperative and affiliative. However, as the group becomes more acculturated in the mainstream, there is more evidence of field independence (Kagan &

Zahn, 1975). Of course, none of this can be substantiated, because of the variation in measures used. The finding observed by a number of Mexican American scholars used the Rod and Frame test, which is a kinesthetic processing task rather than a visual task as used in the study of other cultural groups. It may be that if the visual task such as the Embedded Figures Test had been used, Mexican Americans would have emerged as field independent because the use of visual arts are very prominent in their cultural orientation (Shade, 1989a, b).

Similar observations have been made within the Asian American community. Although it has been suggested that Chinese and Japanese students are highly analytical and prone toward field independence, Timm and Chiang (1997) found that Hmong students tend toward field dependence (field-sensitive style), which they interpreted as reflecting the students' agricultural and socialization practices that emphasize conformity and affiliation.

Conceptual Style

In both the Latino and Hmong communities, the issue of language is important for understanding the conceptual style used. Studies have demonstrated that language, conceptual style, and thinking style are correlated with the culture in which the individual is reared (Trueba, 1988; Trueba, Jacobs, & Kirton, 1990; Valencia, 1991). Each group has its own language symbols that represent the world, and many researchers indicated that thinking patterns emanate from the semantics and grammar used in the native language. Therefore, where languages are similar, concepts have similar meanings; when languages differ, different connections emerge. Garcia (1991) found that when given the opportunity to process information in their own language and at their own speed, Mexican American children are able to learn and think at very high levels.

Thinking Style

The success of people from Eastern cultures in mathematics and the use of technology tends to suggest a preference for the field independent, analytical style of processing information. Stigler and Baranes (1988) suggested that this style may be embedded in Asian cultures in language as well as in the tools and symbols they use. Dao (1991) suggested that the style evolves because there is a heavy emphasis on rote learning and memory. Whether because of the visual arts instruction or the socialization and requirement that they attend to the directions of their elders and people in authority, it is evident that many Asian children are exposed to the sequential approach to processing information. They are able to attend to and assimilate details.

Summary

Culture appears to influence the approach and strategies individuals use in processing information, particularly in the types of modalities used, the cues to which attention is paid, and thinking styles. Teachers interested in mediating differences to improve learning performance must plan for these variations when designing instruction. Suggestions on how these accommodations can be made are discussed in the forthcoming chapters.

ACTION STEP III

You have now examined learning from the perspective of different cultural groups in your classroom. You are the balancer and bridge between those cultures. Examine the various tenets of school cognitive style and compare them to the styles suggested here.

QUESTION: How does the community cultural cognitive style fit with the school cognitive style?

School Oriented Style	Community Oriented Style
Perceptual Style: Modalities favored are auditory and visual with print being a primary focus.	
Attentional Style: Prefers a focus on the task or the object.	
Attentional Style: Prefers introversion-orientation toward inner self and objects.	
Conceptual Style: Has taxonomic categories with universal meanings. Considers functional categories as inappropriate.	
Conceptual Style: Prefers disjointed or decontextualized information and facts.	
Thinking Style: Prefers field-independent way of processing.	

Questions: 1. Do the cognitive styles in your classroom form a continuum?

2. What changes can you make in your classroom and teaching to build bridges to knowledge for all students based on their cognitive styles?

SUGGESTED READINGS

Bruner, J. (1960). *The process of education.* New York: Vintage Books.

Guild, P. B., & Garger, S. (1985). *Marching to different drummers.* Washington, DC: Association of Supervision and Curriculum Development.

Hale, J. (1982). *Black children: Their roots, culture, and learning styles.* Provo, UT: Brigham Young University Press.

Hollins, E. R. (1996). *Culture in school learning.* Mahwah, NJ: Erlbaum.

Kochman, T. (1981). *Black and White: Styles in conflict.* Chicago: University of Chicago Press.

Lazear, D. (1991). *Seven ways of knowing.* Palatine, IL: Skylight Publishing.

Rameriz, M., & Castenada, A. (1974). *Cultural democracy, bicognitive development and education.* New York: Academic Press.

goal 4

Identifying Ways to Structure a Culturally Compatible Classroom

This section provides examples of classrooms and a review of the suggestions made by experts in the field on how a classroom can be reorganized to build cultural bridges between the school culture and the culture of the community from which students come. The goal of this section is to illustrate a culturally compatible classroom for African American, bilingual, and American Indian students.

THE PRACTICE OF CULTURALLY RELEVANT TEACHING

> Children, no matter what their style, fail primarily because of systematic inequities in delivery of any pedagogical approach.
>
> —Asa G. Hilliard III

The most salient and important variable in a student's education is the teacher. Teachers establish the climate, define the tasks, communicate the expectations, help translate the content, monitor understanding, determine the time frame for work completion, and serve as the guide, coach and facilitator throughout the learning process. Of critical importance is the duty of the teacher to establish the psychological climate in which the teaching–learning process takes place. The students often perceive themselves and their capabilities through the eyes of the teacher and he or she communicates the message of student efficacy. Through these efforts, teachers build bridges to knowledge.

Building Bridges to Knowledge

The purpose of the educational process in American schools is to transmit knowledge and information in three areas:

Area 1 is the area of general skills that are needed for survival. This includes the development of literacy (reading, writing, speaking, listening) in the dominant language and the mastery of mathematical skills and processes.

Area 2 includes cultural information that is seen as important to being able to participate in the mainstream of American society. This area includes science, geography, civics, history, and art forms. Again, the determination of what is included is specified by the majority of the society.

Area 3 focuses on expected cultural behavior or cultural norms such as competition and cooperation, individualism and collectivism, reticence and expressiveness, formality and informality, and interactional and interpersonal interactions. These values, as previously mentioned, are reflected in the climate, policy, and procedures designed to enforce cultural style perceived as important.

A difference of opinion now exists between non-White ethnic communities and the schools over what is important in each of these three areas and how the material should be taught. From the perspective of many people of color, there are other ways of teaching the material that build on the strengths of the learning styles of their children. They further suggest that the content in areas 2 and 3 is deficient because it does not include the range of perspectives that incorporate their experiences, ideas, worldviews, and customs.

Educators, on the other hand, suggest that the defined curriculum and strategies are absolute and that the reason the children are not engaged is because they lack motivation, language, and even intellectual capabilities to perform. It is their contention that the families and children must change.

As the success of the KEEP project demonstrated, this is not a war that needs to be waged because it is not an "either/or" situation. The teacher can build the bridges necessary to allow students to maintain their self respect and allegiance while becoming a productive citizen. The key is to find ways to incorporate preferred ways of knowing and children's cultural and lifestyle experiences in ways that entice full participation. Hollins (1996) calls this *culturally mediated instruction*, which means that school practices are an extension of the cultural knowledge from the students' home culture; the curriculum is based on knowledge valued by the students' community and includes the history and culture of the group; and the instructional strategies are congruent with their cognitive styles.

As you examine each of the scenarios in this chapter, identify in your journal some ideas that can become a regular part of your classroom practices.

AN AFROCENTRIC CLASSROOM

My double sized classroom with a portable room divider is located near the media center. My room is airy and inviting with African American colors of red, black, and green that set the tone for high expectations, pride, sense of belonging, and academic excellence. Our day begins with my welcome to 24 students at the door with an African greeting of *Jambo* or *Harambe*. The students sit at tables for four, arranged in a semicircle to face me and wait expectantly for our affirmation period, which sets the tone for each day. Jason Johnson is the griot for today.

Jason asks the group to stand and hold hands.

GRIOT: Greetings, Brothers and Sisters.
CLASS: Greetings, Griot. (Group claps three times.)
GRIOT: Today's affirmation is "Mistakes are a fact of life. It is the response to error that counts." —Nikki Giovanni .
CLASS: (Individual students interpret what the affirmation means to them and for the work they must do for the day. They also relate how the affirmation will help them to be successful in their respective tasks.)
GRIOT: The Griot is finished.
CLASS: Thank you, Griot. (Group claps three times.)

The students then move to their respective learning areas and our day begins. Lewis Walker strolls in late and retreats to an area that is set aside for students who need some time out and aren't ready to participate. The area contains a small refrigerator, a hot pot, and a microwave for students who need food to enhance their abilities to learn. It is also a place for quiet reflection. As I walk toward him, he begins to fix himself a cup of cocoa. I review the affirmation with him and we discuss together how he can apply it to his tasks for the day.

The classroom space is divided into three main instructional areas; the smaller area has one rectangular and one round table, each of which seats about eight students. Sarah Brown, Josie Little, and Morris Hicks identify possible African American personalities that they will portray in the "Ebony Notables" performance planned for next month. The table is soon covered with a variety of academic resources on science, math, philosophy, history, economics, and geography. The students engage in a discourse. They sit in close proximity and use their bodies and gestures to persuade each other on the merits of their particular choices. Bookcases line one wall and contain African, African American, and other multicultural world literature. Prints of Clementine Hunter and Jacob Lawrence hang above the bookcases. Replications of sculptures by Gwendolyn Knight Lawrence rest directly beneath. A comfortable couch is off to one side under a wide expanse of window sills where many pots of geraniums, hibiscus, chrysanthemums, and other species of plants bloom throughout the year. Roderick Bailey and Jessica Adams lounge at opposite ends of the couch. Roderick wears headphones to listen to Beethoven and silently reads *Why We Can't Wait* by Martin Luther King. Jessica appears pensive as she takes notes while she reads the *Autobiography of Malcolm X*. The two students are preparing for a debate on the philosophies of these two great leaders of the Civil Rights Movement.

The second space contains 10 computer stations with desk space for two students at each station. Groups of students work on a variety of projects: comparing the cultural geography of Africa and the United States, predicting and graphing the seasonal migration of birds through information found on the Internet, and writing to a textbook editor with critiques of the lack of information on ancient African scholars within the text. Cassettes and videos are also located in this technological area to support a variety of learning styles. Jeremy Lawler and Inez Stewart classify African American music from the late 1800s to the present, which is part of the "Ebony Notables" performance. Their task is to identify the common themes in the musical styles of the past and present. Jeremy and Inez sway in unison as their hands drum the rhythms on the table. Student artwork and autobiographical sketches depict contributions from African American writers, scientists, and political leaders form a prominent display on the back wall.

The third space is much larger, with tables arranged so that groups of four students can sit in clusters to facilitate different grouping strategies and facilitate cooperative learning. Resources in this area include a chalkboard, science materials, and displays of the seven Nguza Saba Principles (Kwanza) and the Cardinal Virtues of Ma'at (Ancient Egypt). The fourth wall contains a student classroom management wheel that encourages cooperative groups and individual and group responsibilities. It also contains illustrations of mathematical concepts and a display lists the students' content standards and performance expectations for achievement. During this period, the tables are used to create a theater area where the rest of the students are practicing their individual parts for the "Ebony Notables." The backdrop scenery consists of student impressions of well-known and important unknown contributors that represent the total African American experience. As Kerry Robinson portrays W. E. B DuBois, Erica Wells videotapes him, while the rest of the students use a rubric to provide feedback to Kerry to help him prepare for his performance on the big day.

Our day ends the way it began with our griot. As we hold hands, the griot asks the students to close their eyes and repeat the affirmation for the day. The griot asks them to reflect and visualize their day and their completed tasks. They reflect silently for 2 minutes. We close by repeating "Harambe" seven times with our hands extended in the air. This signifies our unity, purpose, and sense of responsibility to each other. I feel tired, but very satisfied.

STOP AND REFLECT VII | **Examine the Afrocentric Classroom**

Consider the following questions:

1. How is this classroom different from most classrooms? Why is this important?

2. What social patterns are evident? What can you infer about the students as a result of these patterns?

3. In what ways does the teacher accommodate the cognitive differences of her students? How might you make this classroom more effective?

4. What next steps further define the scenario of these African American students' view of the world? What next steps would you take to refine or expand further these world views?

STOP AND REFLECT VII | **(CONT'D)**

5. What elements of the scenario provoke cognitive dissonance for you as the reader? What question would you most like to ask at this point? What question would you want someone to answer for you at this point?

6. How would you describe the teaching style of this teacher?

7. What factor in the climate most directly affects student achievement? Why?

Developing an Afrocentric Classroom

African American children arrive in the classroom in which there are generally preconceived notions of who they are and what they can do. However, these children are not individuals who have been inadequately socialized by their families or who have cognitive deficits. They are people with African connections, not just in color, but in habits of mind, actions, and perceptions. Herskovitz (1939) made the observation that most people who teach African Americans do not give the slightest thought to the possibility that there was retention of African thought and speech that might influence the reception of the instruction offered.

Children of African descent come from a tradition of formal education. Weinberg (1977) reports that the Muslim tradition of West Africa from which many of the slaves were obtained inculcated a high value of education, regardless of social class. More important, the process of education was different than that of Anglo-Europeans. Instead of print, knowledge was transmitted orally through the griot tradition, apprenticeships, and basic adult–child interaction. Children learned through observation and within the context of living rather than the accumulation of abstract, decontextualized facts.

African American life in the New World began with the voyages of African explorers from Nubia and Mali (Sizemore, 1990). Many Africans accompanied the other explorers including Columbus and brought with them knowledge of navigation, agriculture, and mining. Within their country there existed many universities including the Songhay learning centers. African Americans come from a tradition of learning. Unfortunately, the slave trade destroyed this tradition and brought people and their subsequent offspring to a society with an intense emotional reaction to their skin color. Edward Shils (1967) described the impact of color as one that seems to generate a psychological obsession. He noted,

> Color by itself is meaningless. It is not like religion, which is a belief and entails either voluntary or hereditary membership. . . . It is not like kinship, which is a tangible structure in which the individual has lives . . . It is not like intellectual culture which is a belief and an attitude toward the world. It is not even like nationality . . . Color is just color. It is a physical, spectroscopic fact . . . Yet it attracts the mind. (p. 279)

This obsession permeates American society and has set the stage for the types of assumptions that often imply, both verbally and nonverbally, that African American children cannot learn. More important, previously established policies and practices have created a set of psychological and social beliefs that African American children do not need an effective education.

To build bridges and invite a larger percentage of African American children to the learning table begins with acceptance of the history of African American people and their strengths. From the examination of studies of academically successful African American individuals, one of the authors (Shade, 1978) found that these individuals:

◻ Have strong will and inner discipline and were in strong control of themselves;

◻ Have strong determination and perseverance in spite of frustration;

◻ Have strong motivation and desire to achieve and be successful;

◻ Have realistic goals tempered with flexibility;

◻ Are curious and very goal oriented;

◻ Have a great deal of self-confidence and a good self-concept;

◻ Perceive themselves to be in control of their own future, but do not deny the existence of racism and its impact on their lives;

◻ Are prepared to get along with a minimum of social support from their peers;

❏ Are rather cautious, controlled, and less trusting of the people and situations with which they come in contact;

❏ Are willing to conform to adult demands if they have very positive views of authority figures;

❏ Have a strong belief that they will accomplish their goals.

Individuals who are high academic achievers generally have some type of positive support in their community, church, or family or a combination of all three. The case studies of the high achievers in the '40s and '50s suggested that they had a strong racial identity (Shade, 1978); however, studies by Fordham and Ogbu (1986; Fordham, 1988) of students who achieved in current times suggest that they lack this type of support and their achievement is interpreted as "acting White."

The issue of identity is an important one for all students, and particularly for African Americans because it establishes the psychological reference points and ability to cope with the discrimination and prejudice to which all African Americans are subjected. As Schmeck and Meier (1984) and Cantor and Kihlstrom (1981) pointed out, self-concept or self-reference is an important cognitive dimension. It sets the stage for what you know, what you want to know, and how you interpret what you see. From an educational perspective, students must have a sense of who they are to know what they want from the educational process. Otherwise, they will not spend time in an alien culture like the school or attempt to master ideas and concepts that are considered foreign or incompatible to their interests, their needs, and themselves.

Joyce King (1994) believes that classrooms can be responsive to African American students and academically enhancing if they

1. Enable students to recognize and affirm their collective identification with people of African descent.

2. Give students an enhanced sense of mutual responsibility for their own learning and the learning of their peers. They should also be taught and encouraged to use their knowledge for the benefit of their community, the society, and humanity.

3. Include humanistic and personally meaningful curriculum in all areas particularly from the African American cultural ethos such as proverbial wisdom; metaphoric language; emphasis on African orality; public performance; artistic expression in music, dance, drama, and visual arts; and the humanistic values in math and science.

4. Assist students to recognize and maintain the cultural values and style of the African American community. As such, children must discover, understand, and use the strengths of their cultural patterns in the teaching–learning process.

5. Involve students in critical thinking and inquiry, particularly around the strengths, weaknesses, and difficulties facing their community and society.

Janice Hale (1982), in her early work, examined the culture and learning styles of African American children and suggested several important factors that needed to be included in a culturally congruent educational program. She believes there should be high affective support, which includes small group learning, peer tutoring, and heterogeneous groupings that resemble a family. In addition, work tasks and instruction should develop self-concept, provide opportunities for creative expression, expose children to African and African American culture and traditions, provide opportunities to explore the community, and have experiences that broaden their understanding of the broader community. She also encourages teachers to change the talking time around so that children have equal talk time and they also have the opportunity to hear music while they work. These factors indicate that there are aspects of the home and community culture that can be incorporated without changing any of the goals and purposes of schooling. Although Hale's approach was aimed at children in early childhood classes, many people have found that the factors are just as effective for older children.

An example of this approach to schooling is found in the Afrocentric Educational Academy for middle school youth in Minneapolis, Minnesota. The class taught by Mr. John Cearnal-Poole and Mrs. Grace H. Rogers incorporates many of these dimensions. One that works well is the use of the griot concept.

The word *griot* (pronounced grē-ō) has become popular throughout West Africa as a name for an expert in oral performance. You may recall from the studies of Shirley Brice Heath and Thomas Kochman that the concept of performance is an important part of African American culture (Heath, 1983; Kochman, 1981). The griot in African society is skilled in storytelling and serves the function of poet, historian, teacher, singer, and entertainer. The griot role is used by teachers to

1. Give the students turns to serve as the griot and as such have the opportunity for the collective memory experience of the group in a culturally specific manner.

2. Afford the student leader the opportunity to practice commanding an audience.

3. Teach the student the value of remembering and presenting knowledge that is essential to the survival (successful achievement) of the group within the classroom culture.

4. Enhance the student's self-esteem by giving her or him a significant role in the teaching–learning process.

5. Improve student presentation skills such as use of voice, body, and eye contact as well as oral communication skills.

6. Prove a performance-based outcome and assessment.

7. Include culturally specific information to affirm the group's particular cultural style.

In addition to the use of the griot approach, these teachers incorporated the concepts of cooperation and self responsibility by assigning students different tasks that were related to classroom organization and management. Students were receptionists, timekeepers, couriers, distributors of work and materials, collectors of work, room inspectors, and board maintenance people.

Students assume and perform these roles for a 5-day period and are evaluated while they are being performed through goal sheets, journal entries, and pre- and post-evaluations. In addition to building a sense of community, this approach accentuates feelings of pride, dignity, honor, trust, and reliability. It also provides the opportunity for students to see their classmate's strengths and abilities and increases motivation for excellence. Each of these techniques represent ways of motivating African American youth by capitalizing on their cultural orientations, while stressing the academic content skills they must learn.

A lesson plan used by Mr. Cearnal-Poole and Mrs. Rogers, developed using the griot role, is shown in Exhibit 2:

The principles of cooperation and performance was used by George Cureton in his work designed to improve the reading skills of African American youth in New York City. It worked. He developed with teachers an action approach to reading that focused on teaching reading through phonics through the use of choral reading, call and response techniques, demonstrations, and performance as well as kinesthetic instruction. For example, in the lesson reported (Cureton, 1978), the teacher taught the concept of blending by having children slide around the room. This was done to demonstrate physically how letters and sounds are blended together into the word. Children also slid objects or pictures of objects together.

Learning objectives:
1. Recite previous day's learning focus
2. Recall significant events, people, ideas, values, assignments
3. Recall significant activities the group experienced
4. Use group responses, calls, and claps to heighten level of group participation and learning.

Learning essentials:
1. Recognize and clue a cultural-specific role and performance ritual to enhance the group's knowledge and interconnectedness
2. Use specific language and decorum
3. Include in daily classroom routine
4. Involve the whole group in acts of remembering, affirming and valuing individual and group learning.

Script: (griot stands in front of group)
Opening: Griot: Greetings, Brothers and Sisters
                Class: Greetings, Griot (Group claps 3 times)
                Griot: (Recalls previous day's experiences)
                      Yesterday we . . .
Ending: Griot: The griot is finished.
                Class: Thank you griot. (Group claps 3 times)

Cueing tips for memory:
Have the students write objectives, focus questions, and activities such as homework assignments, vocabulary, etc. daily in notebooks.

The last stage of acquisition of blending skills was taught through a game. The teacher called out a series of code words and the students synthesized the sounds represented by the words and blended them into words. For example, the teacher called out *soap, money, apple, shoe* and the class responded *smash.* The game not only helps the students understand blending but also helps them develop listening skills and relate the sound of the letters to the alphabet. The game is enlarged to have students write the letter as well as responding orally.

The description of the quick, easy, and active interaction between teacher and student is an example not only of the equal-time concept Hale suggested, but is also an example of the verve or variability and fast pace Boykin advocated. The important fact about the strategy is that it increased the scores of the students on standardized tests. Not only were students learning to read, they were also involved in learning speaking, listening, and writing, which is the hallmark of being a literate person.

The teacher perceived by Cureton (1978) to be the most successful with the children was the one who incorporated and recognized Black English and used a rhythmic form of verbal play to encourage children to do their best, to speak, and to listen. This finding suggests that literacy skills are best learned when cultural communication styles are incorporated into instruction. Farr (1986) reviewed the literature in this area of language, culture, and writing and arrived at the same conclusion. Some of the cultural habits that have an impact on literacy development are as follows:

1. African American children place high reliance on context, particularly non-verbal cues, as they negotiate language interactions with other members of their community. Thus, they learn to be flexible and adaptable in their use of language, to switch roles, to imitate, to engage in creative verbal play, and use metaphors and similes. This suggests that the use of the literature approach to reading, role playing, drama, and other interactive strategies should be effective instructional strategies (Heath, 1983).

2. Not only are there differences in semantics noted in the use of Standard English and Black English vernacular in the community, there is a cultural difference in the form and function or meanings attached to words that have definite cultural dimensions. Michaels, Cazden, and Smitherman (cited in Farr, 1986) also described cross-cultural differences in the organization of speaking and language that occurs between the African American and Anglo-European cultures. Whereas mainstream discourse is aimed at topic-centered narratives that focus on one topic and talk about the event and the time, African American children are more likely to be involved in topic branching or topic associating narratives, which expands the topic based upon various other topics that are included. Erickson (1984) noted that there is logic in this approach that is missed by people outside of the culture but it is organized on the basis of audience–speaker interaction rather than a linear sequential style. This approach is also used in writing.

To accommodate these stylistic differences and still motivate African American children to adopt the dialect of wider communication, scholars suggest exposing the students to reading, writing, speaking, and listening in the new mode on a regular basis. This requires teacher-modeling of the semantics, grammar, pragmatics, and discourse flow in the new dialect; it does not mean drilling in grammar, workbooks, and short-answer questions (Palinscar & Brown, 1986). This approach does not imply that African American language will be demolished or degraded. The suggestions indicate a method of transition and bicultural development.

Other suggestions include the use of the writing workshop approach in which children begin composing before they learn mechanics. The students write on topics of their own choosing and they read each others' work. The use of dialogue journals and the involvement of meaningful interaction such as the use of extensive letter writing are also effective tools. Again, the use of these strategies has resulted in increased achievement.

Language usage is also important in the teaching of mathematics because language shapes mathematical thinking as well as the perception of visual, spatial, and symbolic properties. Claudette Bradley and associates (Bradley, Basam, Axelrod, & Jones, 1990) pointed out the difference in both thinking style and vocabulary of the Navajo as it relates to width, length, depth, and other mathematical concepts. Some researchers have proposed that the Asian languages and number names actually provide greater ability to conceptualize mathematical concepts (Bower, 1987; Stigler & Baranes, 1988). Although Baugh (1994) disagrees with the study done by Orr (1987), there is some reason to believe that linguistic differences have an impact on the achievement of African Americans in developing mathematical concepts.

Instructional strategies like those used in the Algebra Project (Moses, Kamii, Swap, & Howard, 1989) make a connection between mathematics and the community or real world. An increased use of hands-on and experiential learning opportunities, more classroom discussion that models and discusses reasoning, the problem solving approach, and more frequent use of cooperative groups and peer support systems would facilitate the communication process necessary to understand mathematics. The important idea to remember is that mathematics is a culturally transmitted body of knowledge and like language, the students from various communities come to school having learned to handle quantitative data within their communities and their lives. Unfortunately, there is a perception that the mathematics of the school has little to do with reality (Stigler & Baranes, 1988).

The suggestion for change in mathematics teaching is best described as a change toward constructivist teaching, in which the model of learning is not based on the traditional direct instruction of concept introduction, practice, application, and further exploration, but on a student-centered learning cycle. Here students begin by experiencing the concepts, then they are introduced to new terms and ways of thinking, and then they reach a stage of discovery and further exploration. The teacher guides, questions, and helps the exploration; students invent and share their results and their reasoning approaches; and finally, students apply their concepts. This more global, holistic nonlinear approach to mathematics is more closely akin to the preferred African American cognitive style (see Exhibit 3).

STOP AND REFLECT VIII	Compare Classrooms

Return to the scenario of the Afrocentric classroom. Identify the recommended dimensions in this classroom. What are the differences in this classroom methods and approaches from your perception of a traditional classroom? From your classroom?

DEVELOPING A BILINGUAL CLASSROOM

Language is not only a source of communication, it also represents an individual's heritage, culture, and feelings. Therefore, maintaining one's native language has an affective dimension that cannot be ignored (Williams & Snipper, 1990). Moreover, as Johnson and Johnson (1994) pointed out, this country has always been a pluralistic and diverse society, not only as it relates to people, but in its food, language, customs, music, art, and literature. America has adopted and adapted something from each of the diverse cultures that exist within the nation. As these authors pointed out, being an American is creedal rather than racial or ancestral. Therefore, schools within this society are charged with the responsibility of (a) helping students maintain their identity with the cultural, ethnic background; (b) developing an appreciation for others cultural, religious, or ethnic backgrounds; (c) developing a superordinate identity as *Americans*; and (d) developing a set of values around democracy, freedom, liberty, equality, justice, the rights of individuals, and the responsibilities of citizenship that fosters the American tradition of strength through diversity. These are important goals for all students, but most important for students whose learning experiences began in a language other than English. The classroom that addresses these goals is a very different classroom than is traditionally conceived.

A Bilingual Perspective

> What a great language I have, it's a fine language we inherited from the fierce Conquistadors. . . . They carried everything off and left us everything. . . . They left us the words.
>
> —Pablo Neruda

I see the excitement and expectation on Manuel's face and I ask, "What words describe what you feel inside the box?" The sun is shining in through the windows of our classroom but the air still feels cool and dry. I detect a smell that's like peppery spices coming from the box. Manuel's eyes raise up to look at the ceiling as he ponders his response in English. "It's cold. It's soft. It feels like it's moving!" Manuel's inserts his hand into the opening in the front of a large green cardboard box. The opening is approximately four inches in diameter.

An open-ended tubular knit piece of material covers the opening so that students can insert their hands to determine what is inside the box without seeing what the box contains. Three other brightly colored boxes with different objects in them rest on the round table in the science laboratory of our classroom. Pairs of students with various levels of English proficiency try to describe and identify the objects in the "mystery boxes." Their task is to use vocabulary words to reflect all of their senses except taste.

On the other side of the table, Pablo asks Ouan to describe what the object sounds like. Ouan quietly whispers, "It rattles. It sounds like a gourd with seeds. My family uses the gourd. We make music."

The science lab is defined by a long row of 3-foot-high bookcases located under a bank of windows. Two large salt water and fresh water aquaria sit on top of the bookcases. Different species of colorful fish and underwater life fascinate the students. Students also have designed a variety of terraria to portray different habitats and study the effect of the environment on different communities of animals. On the wall behind the table in the science lab hang student pictures of various kinds of plants and animals that are found in the children's native countries of Mexico and Laos. The students have labeled them in Hmong, Spanish, and English.

Other bookcases and storage cabinets define many nooks and crannies for learning laboratories so that students can explore a variety of English concepts and reflect on their connection to real world experiences. The nooks and crannies provide an opportunity for self discovery, which is an important strategy to help ESL students develop meaningful understanding.

Around the corner from the science lab is our fine arts laboratory. Mrs. Dao, the ESL teacher, works with a group of 10 students. The students work together to learn a song to reinforce their spelling words for the week. They have created their own musical instruments. For example, Pao and Kia built drums and drumsticks by inserting pencils into large marshmallows to tap on elaborately decorated oatmeal boxes. Rosita and Pablo designed a xylophone by using bottles filled with various levels of water and small hammers made from wood, plastic, aluminum, and rubber. Ms. Dao uses mnemonic strategies to teach the children vowels. She has them learn a rhythm pattern and chant the letters to the beat of their instruments. Ms. Dao also uses the piano and native instruments to help my students learn vowels by listening to the notes and holding their long and short vowel sounds.

A video camera is also located in the fine arts lab for taping individual and group performances to monitor progress in language acquisition. Storytelling, rhymes, limericks, and jokes help students learn new sounds in a fun way. To enhance the oral language focus, this center also provides a natural forum to share cultural celebrations through music, song, dance, and drama. A puppet theater and stage for marionettes provides opportunities for the students to write short plays, create characters and design sets, and perform through media rather than in front of an audience. This lab is stocked with crayons, colored chalk, clay, tempera paint, multicolored construction paper, poster board, and other art supplies to reinforce multisensory learning.

The next nook is the writing laboratory in which one wall covered with student-designed comic strips in Hmong and Spanish. The comic strips are a blend of reality and fantasy. The artwork is very detailed, precise, vivid in color, and somewhat geometric in nature. The comic strips depict a common theme of family life with self-portraits of the students and their extended families included in some fashion in each comic strip. One title reads, "The Family That Won't Quit."

Underneath the comic strip display are shelves with student portfolios and journals that demonstrate student efforts. Samlong, Luis, and Joe are busy writing and editing a class newspaper article about a student survey they have conducted to compare and contrast favorite American and native foods. Preliminary results indicate that students eat a variety of ethnic types of flatbread and no matter what the origin of the culture, pizza still takes first place as their favorite.

Another wall of the writing lab portrays a poster listing the steps necessary to revise and edit written work. I have found another important teaching strategy is to challenge students to critique and make constructive suggestions for improvement of each other's written work. We have designed a simulation where students submit their work to different "publishing companies" and at least three "editors" need to review their work. The "editors" send their constructive responses to the "authors" through an electronic mail system. The "authors" then revise their work, publish it, and submit it to the "KidsWorks" Library.

The final nook is a combined book and game laboratory where Juanita, Luz, and Hue converse with Pablo Martinez from the Chicano El Centro Community Center. Community members volunteer to work with the students to develop English oral skills through a variety of games like "Fish," "Sea of Vowels," and "Where in the World is Consonant City?" Card games and board games draw students to this center for ongoing reinforcement of syllabication, phonics, thinking strategies, and comprehension skills. Ongoing tournaments are held with winners selecting a favorite book to read and then taking the book home to their families to share. Students take turns reading aloud and I often use the chalkboard to diagram the plot, the characters, and the setting while they read. This creates a story map that gives them a visual organizer for important concepts. This integrates both global and analytic processes of their brains because some languages are more pictorial and others are more semantic in nature. Some literature selections include Spanish, Hmong, and English versions of the same book. This gives the students the opportunity to compare and share cultural nuances of the story line, which gives them new insights to themselves and their friends.

I continue to work hard to create a climate of academic challenge, interdependence, trust, choice, and celebration of diversity. Hopefully, the climate of our classroom reflects this. My students deserve nothing less!

The above scenario provides an example of the type of culturally responsive classroom which many teachers and scholars such as Igoa (1995), Williams and Snipper (1990), Hernandez (1993), Garcia (1991), and Cummins (1992) recommend for students who must become competent performers in English as well as their native language. *Bilingualism* implies that students are proficient in understanding a message in each of the languages spoken, are able to respond in each of the languages in a manner appropriate to the situation, are able to read and understand a written message, and are able to write in each language. The more adept people are at performing the four skills in each of the languages, the greater is their level of bilingualism. Cummins and Swain (1986) suggested that bilingualism increases a person's awareness of language and also provides the skills and ability to process information and experiences from two different perspectives.

A caveat: Becoming literate in two languages is not the only concern of immigrant children. Whether the children have arrived because the family perceives increased opportunities or because of political upheaval, children experience emotional stress from being uprooted and moved to a new culture and land. Learning cannot occur until this anxiety has been addressed. Igoa (1995) stressed that the first step in improving academic achievement is to develop a culturally agreeable community of learners. Until children feel a sense of belonging, they cannot use their energies to learn.

Teachers who wish to assist limited English proficiency (LEP) students should first attempt to acquire some of the language of their students themselves, even if only a few words. This will help students realize that their language is acceptable and not inferior. It will also provide more motivation for them to learn to communicate in a new language. Students should also be encouraged to participate in translation opportunities as a way of developing interlanguage skills. Of most importance is allowing the students to determine which language they wish to use to initiate conversation. They will select the one that they consider their best language and it will enhance their academic self-concept (Garcia, 1991). Although students will probably choose English for conversation with the teacher because they recognize this is the language through which they achieve the most, they do not wish to lose their native language as this is probably the language used to communicate with the adults in their community. Maintaining their native language is a badge of community and family loyalty and to become "english only" is a sign of betrayal and rejection of their heritage, culture, and ancestors.

The primary goal of schools for children whose first language is not English is to help the students become biliterate, bicultural, self-directed learners. This is best accomplished if there is good communication between the teacher and students as well as between student and student. Hernandez (1993) suggested that this communication process is best facilitated by using the student's primary language in cognitively challenging ways to focus on the acquisition of content knowledge and from the content develop the understanding and use of the second language. Hernandez further suggests that LEP students will learn best if the learning is developed within the context of real life and the material is of interest to the students. The use of such strategies as visuals, manipulatives, graphic and advance organizers, whole language, cooperative learning, and journals are recommended highly.

Most writers in the field agree that students develop literacy—reading, speaking, writing, listening—proficiently in two languages if they are able to practice the full range of activities in all four modes. Williams and Snipper (1990) suggested that the literature approach provides an opportunity for social interaction that facilitates growth. For example, teachers might select a story, poem, or fairy tale based on interest or prior experience of the student. Using this item, the teacher would then (a) encourage students to listen while the story is read with lots of illustrations and vocabulary work; (b) encourage students to generate connections between the story and their own experience; (c) ask the students to retell the story as a group, chorally, or in unison; and (d) ask the students to write their own translation of the story or the character. The writing process helps clarify thoughts and builds comprehension, therefore students should also be asked to transcribe stories or write group stories, newsletters, or books. Social interaction, peer review, and encouragment of students in finding ways to speak and write in Language 1 in order to follow the same processes in Language 2 seems to be the underlying philosophy for teaching students who must become bilingual.

Several additional suggestions for working with LEP students have been made by members of the Limited English Program in Minneapolis Public Schools and Mr. Soua Yang (Yang, personal communication, May, 1996.) They encourage teachers to

1. Develop both oral and written instructions for lessons and assignments.

2. Make sure to write (maybe on flip charts) key points, words, phrases, and major details that teachers want LEP students to remember.

3. Use lots of visuals and simplify the language of the presentations—not the concepts.

4. Talk slower, not louder, and use body language and visuals to enhance comprehension.

5. Consider having each student develop his or her own vocabulary booklet of difficult words. (Igoa, 1995, also suggested this be included as part of their homework book.)

6. Create a literate environment. Allow LEP students to see and hear lots of language in a variety of ways. Igoa (1995) suggested that the use of art and music of a student's native land can be important tools for enhancing this environment.

DEVELOPING A CLASSROOM FOR AMERICAN INDIANS

The following suggestions represent ideas proposed by researchers and educators interested in enhancing the teaching of American Indian students. They suggest that culturally responsive teachers should

1. Gain insight into the history of each tribe as a way of gathering knowledge about their ways of thinking.

2. Capitalize on the propensity for giving and sharing through the use of cooperative learning techniques. Native American children need to feel a part of the group as though they are members of a family or a tribe.

3. Where possible, use their language and symbols.

4. Use natural phenomena when planning science lessons because nature and the supernatural are important values for Native Americans.

5. Integrate dance, art, legends, and folktales where possible. These media can greatly facilitate reading, language arts, speaking, writing, social studies, and the development of critical thinking.

6. If teachers wish Native American students to participate in classroom activities, it is important to use open-ended questions, equal talk time, intuitive and analytical reasoning, and tacit learning experiences.

It is also noted that strategies suggested for use with potential bilingual students are just as important for Native American children as they are for immigrants or other LEP students (see Exhibit 4).

The following scenario provides some insight into how these suggestions might be incorporated:

Exhibit 4	A Teaching Style That Works With Native-American Learners

1. Use cooperative learning groups rather than traditional grouping;
2. Provide a high percentage of group projects and low percentage of oral questions and answers;
3. Incorporate manipulative devices and activities which allow a student to "feel and touch;"
4. Provide variety of informal classroom settings with freedom of movement—studying on the floor, sitting at a table or desks arranged in small groups, etc.;
5. Present the whole picture of things before isolating skills into small segments;
6. Provide activities that are experience based;
7. Provide a high rate of encouragement;
8. Provide mobility through scheduled activities;
9. Provide values-clarification activities;
10. Use peer tutoring and cross-age teaching;
11. Provide artwork illustrating people and animals, cartoons, wood carving, model building, miniature displays, map-making;
12. Use role-playing and creative dramatics;
13. Organize learning center materials to address all the needs of all learners in the classroom;
14. Encourage opinionated expression of viewpoints in social studies and other subjects where controversy can be found;
15. Present new and difficult material in a visual/spatial mode rather than a verbal mode;
16. Use metaphors, images, analogies and symbols rather than dictionary type definitions;
17. Use parades and productions such as "Classroom 20/20" or "News In Review;"
18. Use brainstorming and open-ended activities;
19. Schedule sports and play days;
20. Use instructional games; and
21. Student-designed games are particularly effective.

—Pepper and Henry (1986)

My Classroom for First Americans

A banner hangs from the second floor balcony of my school with the following Native American philosophy:

> This earth is our mother
> She is sacred
> Take from her only
> What you need
> . . . she feeds us
> . . . she clothes us
> . . . she gives us shelter
> Honor Mother Earth
> Protect her
> Take care of her so that she
> May take care of those
> Who will live after us.

Entering the foyer of my school is like entering a traditional Ojibwe Native American village. To my left proudly stands a 10-foot-high teepee with a frame made from sturdy sapling trees. Birch bark and animal skins decorated with hand-painted Ojibwe symbols that have special meaning and tell the story of the history and culture cover the frame of the teepee. From a distance, the teepee appears white with splashes of red, blue, black, and yellow that form the symbols to represent animals and plants. At the entryway, a flap stands open as a welcome to visitors. Displays surround the teepee to show the versatility of birch bark (*weegwahs*): a small canoe, small containers (*muhkuk*) to hold water, fruits, or vegetables, and baskets used for other utilitarian purposes depict the day to day life in a historical Ojibwe village.

To my right is the winter version of an Ojibwe dwelling that is called a *wigwam*. The wigwam is made of bent poles and birchbark to form a dome-like structure. The Ojibwe people used a variety of natural materials for a caulk in order to insulate their homes against the bitter winters. As I move through the village towards my classroom, I think about the resourcefulness of the Ojibwe people in earlier times and how that tradition is still honored today.

Entering my classroom is like entering one of the dwellings in the village. Although the physical structure is not the same as a teepee or a wigwam, the social structure and climate of the room reflect authentic Ojibwe life. The room is organized with a combination of learning center areas, quiet study areas, and a large activity space. Tables and chairs rather than desks are located throughout the many learning centers. The room is bright with a bank of windows that face east. The learning centers are defined by the clustering of tables and chairs in a circle with bookcases and storage cabinets surrounding them.

Near the door of my room hang birchbark calendars inscribed with the months of the year, the weekly moon cycles, and days of the week in both English and Ojibwe. John Thundereagle and Jess Reynolds try to determine what important Ojibwe celebrations need to be added to the calendar. Jim Clark, an elder, is telling them a story about the moon phases and what importance that has to their way of life and survival.

In the science area, Rachel Smith, Ramona Childs, and Jerry Weaver compare the height of different Ojibwe plants that are planted by students in different types of soil. Ojibwe plants include wild rice, corn, squash, pumpkin, wild onion, chokecherry, blueberry, red raspberry, and strawberry. The students must develop a bar graph to show the relationships of the different variables to environmental factors. The students use several kinds of measuring devices as well as microscopes to enrich their observations. On the back wall of the science area, several colorful T-shirts are displayed on a bulletin board covered with Indian weavings. The T-shirts, designed by the students with the help of several community members, depict several themes: Native American foods that we still enjoy today, Native American contributions made to the scientific world, Native American words used in everyday language, and the important animal characters within Ojibwe folktales.

Several students are busy setting up the large area of the room for the KIVA process to be held this afternoon (see p. 123 for a description of this process). We have invited parents, elders, and community members to come and exchange their views about tribal government and Indian sovereignty with us. A difference of opinion between two students on whether Indian people should spearfish and hunt regardless of state law prompted this community dialogue. As the students arrange the tables in an octagonal shape, they are listening to an audio tape of a pow-wow that they attended last month. The rhythm of the drums helps the students work cooperatively and complete the task. The drums are playing very softly and Indian singers chant in a melodic rhythm that is very soothing.

The math area of the room contains games and other manipulatives that develop thinking and support mathematical skill development. Two teams of students are engaged in "game sticks" to help them understand the concepts of patterns, relations, and functions, randomness, uncertainty, and discrete mathematics. The game sticks are made from hollow wood. The sticks are decorated on one side with colorful Native American symbolic designs. The other side is plain. The object of the game is to predict how the sticks will land when thrown into the air. The students must predict first of all, how many sticks will land with their design side up and secondly, what patterns will evolve. The students laugh and their excitement is very evident. Other games found in this center include the bowl game played by the ancient American Indians, the walnut shell game, and the stone warriors game. Students love to compete within a cooperative structure.

Student-made dream catchers and medicine wheels are displayed prominently in the arts and crafts area. Beneath each of these Native American symbols, students have written their explanation of its historical and cultural significance. A few students have combined their dream catchers to create a class mobile that hangs from the ceiling. The students believe that this class mobile will catch all of the bad dreams and entrap them and the good dreams of the class will flow through to the future. The medicine wheel has an even greater spiritual significance. The medicine wheel signifies north, south, east, and west as well as earth, wind, fire, and water. It serves as a foundation for the belief system and values of Native Americans.

In the corner of the arts and crafts center is a pottery wheel and shelves for student designed projects. Coiled clay pots dry on the shelves in the filtered sunlight. As soon as the pottery is dry, students will apply layers of glaze before they are fired in the kiln. Amanda and Joe sit together thinning out a slab of clay with a flat rock. They plan to embed a pictograph story on their clay tablet. The storage shelves of the arts and crafts center contain multiple sizes of beads made of different natural materials; a variety of fabrics and textures; a rainbow of colorful naturally dyed yarns and hemp; and objects from nature, which include containers of shells, pine cones, multicolored agates, dried seeds, and flowers.

The communications center includes an area where Native American folktales and other stories are read and written. A series of study carols provides students with an opportunity to sit quietly and concentrate, write, read, or reflect without distractions. Book shelves line the walls and help define the center. The book shelves hold student journals, a series of Waynaboozhoo legends, Ojibwe folktales, and other Native American and English literature. On top of the bookshelves are many games, which are used to reinforce student conceptual understanding and increase their memory. Two elders, Michael Running Elk and Judy Cutler, work with a small group of students in the technology lab section of the communications center. They have developed the following set of class expectations, which reflect Native American values and beliefs:

Respect: Respect shows honor to all around you. To show respect means to be polite and thoughtful to yourself, others and things around you. We all have gifts and recognize and appreciate those in others.

Harmony: To live in harmony is to live in balance physically, intellectually, emotionally, and spiritually. To live in harmony one must take care of one's self and others. You must cooperate with your community members in order to obtain balance. The honor of one is the honor of all.

Effort: Effort is to do your best in everything you do and to be satisfied with what you have done.

Humor: Humor is to find enjoyment in work, play, and friends. Humor is an element of life. It is a necessary aspect of harmony and of balance. Humor is positive; it is not sarcastic or hurtful.

Dream Weaver: To reach a goal, one must first imagine it. Dream weaving is a process that includes planning, persistence, and commitment. One can be anything one wants to be, but one must first dream. Goals can change, but don't stop dreaming.

Responsibility: Responsibility is taking ownership of your actions. How you act, work, and play affects other people and yourself. Think before you act and be careful.

Safety: Safety is a state of well-being. To feel safe means to know that no one or nothing will hurt you. To feel safe depends on freedom from hurt, put-downs, and an unsafe environment.

After the elders and students have printed this set of expectations on a chart, my class will use them as part of their daily affirmations to establish harmony within themselves and our classroom. I will use these same expectations to reaffirm my commitment to my students and to remind myself that I too am part of the universe. As I review my students accomplishments, I am at peace.

Although the approach may vary depending upon the school and the composition of the classroom, four very important elements are present in a culturally responsive classroom. First, the teacher makes the difference. A teacher who demonstrates warmth, a tolerant attitude, and a determination that all students will acquire the skills they need is one who is successful in a diverse classroom, particularly with students who believe schools are "not for them." A second element is the classroom environment. Classrooms must be stimulating, colorful, and filled with materials that both relate to the students and introduce new ideas and concepts. Third, the social interaction process must be accepted both among students and between teachers and students. Each individual must perceive that she or he is free to assist, free to offer assistance, and free to make personal contact with other students and the teacher. A fourth element and the major way of demonstrating cultural tolerance and acceptance is in the teacher's response to and use of the language that is prevalent within the child's community. Instead of transmitting the message, either verbally or nonverbally, that the language is unacceptable, the teacher must find ways to use this language as a bridge to develop ideas and concepts. These four elements set the stage for success. With this foundation, teachers can develop presentations and interactions that teach, using their own strategies as well as other instructional strategies described in the next Goal.

You have reviewed the classrooms adaptations for three cultural groups, but there were many similar suggestions. List some common ideas to use to make changes in your instructional practices and your classroom that might foster cognitive engagement of students with diverse ways of knowing.

_____

_____

_____

_____

We will explore what you have discovered and continue to expand your repertoire of strategies in the next Goal.

	Action Step IV

How Would You Change?

From a Traditional Classroom	To a Culturally Compatible Classroom
View children as products to be shaped	
Monocultural view	
Focus on whole group needs	
Challenging curriculum for some	
Lecture, text, and demonstrations	
Decontextualized content	
Learner receives information passively	
Silence	
Focus on facts and details	
Teach for recall and memorization	
Textbook centered	
Use of only basal readers	
Seatwork: workbook, worksheets, dittos	
Single-subject focus	
Teacher conveys knowledge	
Teacher is authority	
Question–answer discussion, teacher led	
Tracking of students by ability	
Teach to remediate	
Science: Performing predefined experiments	

	Action Step IV, continued
From a Traditional Classroom	To a Culturally Compatible Classroom
Social Studies: Only one perspective	
Use only societal/teacher examples	
Teacher-centered classroom	
Competitive learning	
Classroom climate is work and business	
English only allowed	
Working and learning alone	
Material presented in linear approach	
Impersonal classroom	
Little peer-to-peer interaction	
Mainstream values only	
Reading taught separately from writing	
Mathematics is memorization of facts	

Questions:
1. Which of these is the easiest to implement? Why?
2. Which of these is the most difficult to implement? Why?

SUGGESTED READINGS

Chinn, A., & Seyer, I. (1994). *Asian-Pacific Americans: Perspectives in history and culture: A teachers' resource book*. Torrance, CA: Frank Schaffer Publications.

Cole, R. W. (Ed.). (1995). *Educating everybody's children: Diverse teaching strategies for diverse learners*. Alexandria, VA: Association of Supervision and Curriculum Development.

Delgado-Gaitan, C., & Trueba, H. (1991). *Crossing cultural borders*. London: Falmer Press.

Igoa, C. (1995). *The inner world of the immigrant child*. New York: St. Martin's Press.

Ladson-Billings, G. (1994). *The dreamkeepers: Successful teachers of African American children*. San Francisco: Jossey Bass.

goal 5

Increasing Knowledge of
Culturally Compatible Strategies

This section puts theory into practice: It provides a summary of the ideas previously presented and shows how they can be implemented in a classroom. The ideas presented include examples used in various culturally oriented schools in the Minneapolis Public School District. These practices work.

"You must be the change you wish to see."

—Mahatma Gandhi

By choosing to read and interact with this material, you began a journey that should transform you and your classroom in ways that reflect diverse world views. As you engage in this process of change, you will find that you have more questions than answers. Among the questions that will emerge are the following:

◻ What is my vision for creating a culturally compatible classroom so that all children can and will learn?

◻ What do I know and how do I find out more about my students and their previous learning experiences?

◻ How do I secure knowledge of the expectations of my school district and community for preparing students for success in the 21st century?

◻ How much knowledge do I have and how much do I need to learn about various cultures and their implications for cognitive styles?

The classroom scenarios provided snapshots of some sample multicultural settings designed to address specific cultural needs of students. Review them again. Examine each with the idea that it can provide an answer to the question, how do I get there and where do I start? Explore these scenarios using our suggestions, which focus on climate, curriculum, and instructional strategies.

CULTURALLY RESPONSIVE ENVIRONMENTS

How do you make your classroom inviting? How do you ensure that your students have a positive sense of belonging and are affirmed? This is critical when designing a culturally compatible environment for students of any age. Students need to see themselves and their cultures reflected through pictures, displays, artifacts, room arrangements, and inclusion of different languages. Every culture values an environment that is welcoming, safe, and creates a positive sense of identity and unity. To create an inviting student-centered classroom that reflects a variety of cultures and interests and provides a sense of belonging, consider the following suggestions:.

◻ *Use color and design.* Purchasing a variety of ethnic cloths, prints, art work, and artifacts.

□ *Create a "Welcome Center" where students can share food.* Research by Rita and Kenneth Dunn (1975) indicated that about 15% of students need a constant intake of food or beverages to maintain high levels of energy. You may need that yourself—where is your coffee cup?

□ *Provide a variety of multimedia to listen to music.* Dunn and Dunn also reported that some students need to have sound in the background to block out other distractions. Additional research shows that music helps to stimulate the brain (Prichard & Taylor, 1978; Ostrander & Schroeder, 1979). In our classrooms, we use cultural music ranging from American Indian flute to Black Legends of Jazz to set the tone for calm reflection, to prepare for tests, to energize, and to increase time on task. Headsets are very helpful!

□ *Plan opportunities for students to express spirituality and creativity.* Dance, visual arts, drama, choral reading, vocal and instrumental music, and graphic arts provide pathways for students to share each others' cultures. These are effective ways to integrate cultural activities into your curriculum so that students can demonstrate their knowledge, talents, and skills.

□ *Build on previous experiences from the students' individual cultures.* Students need to construct their own understanding. This often implies hands-on learning, space for lots of activity, and a climate where students can take risks and have more questions than answers.

□ *Design space with tables and desks so that the majority of students' time is spent in cooperative learning.* The amount of research in support of cooperative learning is overwhelming, but individual and competitive activities are also appropriate and space must be flexible enough to allow such things to happen. Remember to accommodate the differences in your students' learning styles.

□ *Involve students in the planning of your room arrangements.* Change the room often as a way of stimulating those students who are visual and who need to have variety.

□ *Position your desk so that you send a message of collaboration rather than authority.*

□ *Plan long-term and short-term interest centers.* Use light, temperature, formal and informal types of furniture, and motivational materials to accommodate the visual, auditory, and kinesthetic differences in your students. Remember, technology is highly motivating and must be integrated throughout your classroom.

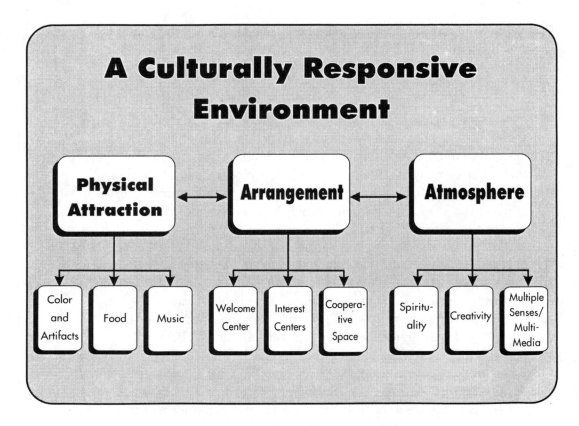

Figure 5

A CULTURALLY RESPONSIVE CURRICULUM

A culturally responsive student-centered curriculum is rich and meaningful because it takes into consideration the experiences, realities, and interests of the students. All lessons must be relevant to the students' lives. Teachers start from students' own experiences and build on them to help students understand new concepts. The belief that all students come to school equipped and prepared with basic experiences and fundamental knowledge is key to this direct method of teaching a diverse population of students whose experiences change on a daily and sometime hourly basis. Aletha Halcomb, a Minneapolis Public Schools physics teacher, has developed a model that she uses as a foundation for her dual assignment as the lead teacher for the Afrocentric Educational Academy and for her high school physics classes. This model has also been adapted for use in elementary multicultural curriculum design and is currently being used by many K–12 teachers throughout the district. Halcomb defined contextual curriculum as using the daily experiences of at least 85% of students in the class to connect what they know to what they need to know to be academically successful.

The foundation of contextual curriculum is the use of questionnaires to examine comprehensively the daily activities, available materials, and community resources within the grasp of a large number of students. This information is used as an entry point to introduce the curriculum concepts to be learned. The process involves

❏ developing survey questions for your population

❏ administering the survey to the class

❏ compiling the responses

❏ developing activities or the selection of predesigned activities that support at least 85% of student responses

Exhibit 5 represents an example of this approach beginning with the survey questionnaire, which can be given to elementary as well as middle and secondary students.

Responses to these questionnaires revealed that 85% of students can cook a meal or warm food. Eighty-eight percent have a microwave oven in their homes, 100% have either a working natural gas or electric stove in their homes, and 96% have access to a refrigerator. Also, 82% have access to a clock, watch, or timer. From this basic information a unit on heat transfer is a natural. Other concepts that flow from this information are the study of waves; different types of materials like the effect of metal, plastic, glass, and wood as conductors or insulators; meteorology and the temperature of stars; skills for measuring and analyzing heat like thermometer reading; timing devices; data collection; and so on.

Exhibit 5 | A Sample Experiential Questionnaire

Which of these items (equipment) do you have in your home on a continuous basis?

___typewriter	___dimmer switch
___audio cassette player	___magnifying glass
___video cassette player/recorder (VCR)	___air conditioner
___camera	___refrigerator
___binoculars	___automobile
___microwave oven	___bicycle
___skate board	___in-line skates
___electric or gas range	___remote control
___telescope	___camcorder VCR
___sewing machine	___thermometer
___musical instrument	___Polaroid camera
___television	___dishwasher
___radio	___computer
___compact disc player	___tape player
___magazines	___thesaurus
___scissors	___dictionary
___tape/paste/glue	___books
___hand tools (saw, drill, hammer, etc.)	___encyclopedia
___sewing materials, thread needles, etc.	___writing paper
___odds and ends of lumber	___pencil/pen
___nails/screws	___Atlas
___board games (chess/checkers)	___puzzles
___Scrabble/Password/Trivial Pursuit	___Rubic's Cube
___Interactive computer games	___battery powered toys
___yo-yo	___rockets
___paints	___slot cards
___battery powered toys	___Etch-A-Sketch
___wind-up toys	___electric trains
___musical toys	___computer games
___models	___airplanes

Note: From the Marcy School Staff, Minneapolis Public Schools. Used with permission.

It is not always necessary to develop new units after reviewing the results of the survey. Sometimes a simple modification of existing units or changing the way the material is presented (e.g., teaching the lesson by beginning with the concrete and proceeding to the abstract) will build relationships to contexts or situations that are familiar to the students.

STYLISTICALLY RESPONSIVE INSTRUCTIONAL STRATEGIES

Teachers must modify instruction to facilitate academic achievement among students from diverse cultural groups. According to James Banks (1990), this results in creating *equitable pedagogy*—using more cooperative learning strategies in class and using the language and understandings that students bring to school to bridge the gap between what students know and what they need to learn. The teacher acknowledges and embraces the students as they are and builds on the experiences that students bring with them as referenced in the contextual curriculum planning. The teacher must show respect for the background and experiences of the students and offer instruction to maintain literacy in the students' main primary language. It is important to engage students actively in the learning process, rather than expect them passively to receive information. The following strategies, as summarized in Figure 6 and portrayed in the scenarios, are effective practices to encourage culturally diverse and culturally specific groups of students.

Cooperative Learning Strategy

Research overwhelmingly supports the use of cooperative learning for all cultural groups as a main strategy in a culturally compatible classroom. The work of Johnson and Johnson (1994), Cohen (1986), and others provide a com-

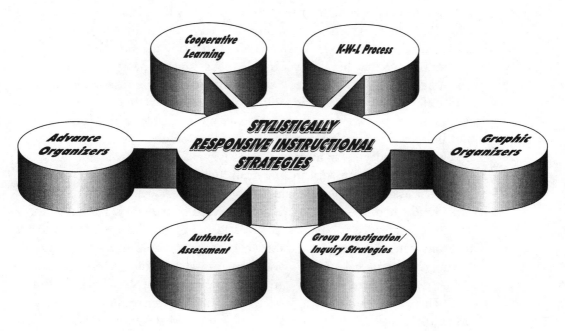

Figure 6

mon direction for the strategy, but each has unique nuances that affect culturally diverse students. The use of group process skills, face-to-face interaction, positive interdependence, social skills, and individual accountability provides opportunities to learn more about each other, build trust, and help each other engage in rigorous academics. For example, cooperative group discussions are used to sharpen student thinking and language skills. Teachers engage students in active exploration of real-life phenomenon and encourage them to test their observation and conclusions. Working in small groups, students must agree on an answer or develop a group product to reflect their work. The teacher listens to the students' approaches to the task and asks questions that make students reflect and strengthen their thinking skills. All of the students must be individually accountable for the knowledge they have acquired and therefore help each other to develop the concepts and skills to demonstrate their work. Please note: Given the impact of the research, it is important that teachers practice the tenets of cooperative learning and not just engage their students in group work. It is also important for teachers to stay current with the most recent developments in this strategy, because it is still evolving.

K-W-L Strategy

A teacher often begins a lesson by asking the students what they know, what they want to know, and upon reflection, what they have learned. This is called a K-W-L strategy, which also is appropriate across all cultural groups. *K* stands for "What do you know?," *W* stands for "What do you want to know?," and *L* stands for "What have you learned?" This strategy has significance when planning for a culturally diverse student population because students bring very different experiences and skills that are rooted in their respective families, cultures, and communities. A teacher must be able to recognize, affirm, and build on students' previous experiences in order to help them bridge to a new idea, concept, or understanding. For example, Mrs. Smith questions Jesse about a book on African American folk tales that he has been reading. When she asks, "What is the main idea of the story?," Jesse responds, "*Umoja.*" Mrs. Smith then says, "I don't recall that word in the story. I want to know what the main idea is." If Mrs. Smith had the cultural knowledge to know that *umoja* means" unity" in Swahili, her response would have been very different. An alternative strategy would be to ask a probing question such as "What do you mean by that?" or "Tell me more about what you are thinking." The probe would cause Jesse to elaborate and share the relationship of his cultural background to the present situation. Mrs. Smith would also realize that Jesse was correct in his response and has a deeper understanding of the complexities of the story than most children in his age group. African American students often use metaphors in their responses, which shows the complexity of their thinking processes.

Group Investigation–Inquiry Strategy

Inquiry strategies are a natural for culturally responsive, student-centered classrooms where students bring diverse cultural perspectives to an issue or question. They require the teacher to play a facilitative role to direct group process, engage the students in inquiry, and function as an academic counselor. The teacher helps the students plan, implement, and manage their own decisions. Diverse opinions, reasons, and negotiations should be allowed and emphasized. This strategy includes the following steps:

1. Students encounter a puzzling situation (planned or unplanned).
2. Teacher and students explore reactions to the situation.
3. Students formulate a study task. They organize to study the situation (problem definition, role, assignments, etc.).
4. Students engage in independent and group study.
5. Teacher and students analyze progress and process.
6. Refine original puzzling situation and recycle through steps.

An example of this strategy is portrayed in A Vision of the Future when the four students are building a terrarium in the science center. Their discovery of the chameleon changing colors may lead to an entire class investigation of the concepts of protective coloration and endangered species. These concepts may provide a very rich and powerful discussion when application is made to the cultural experiences of African American, Hmong, Native American, and Mexican American groups.

This inquiry method and encouragement of student participation also can be successfully used in language arts activities. Students need to be encouraged to produce oral and written language and to relate to the subject matter from their own cultural experience. The teacher understands that students vary in previous schooling, primary language literacy, and trauma level. Some come with no prior school education. For this group the teacher asks students to use their own experience to generate stories. Students would then make up stories and develop vocabulary lists, generate words, draw pictures, and use the words and pictures to build literacy. They also create their own oral folk tales written in their own native language. Language arts inquiry and investigative group processes also may include interviewing people in their community, welcoming parents and community members into the classroom in innovative ways, and establishing communication through technology with the broader community. These activities demonstrate a commitment to help students maintain their primary language. Such an approach provides a connection to their home country and indicates to students that their language and culture are valued.

Advance Organizers Strategy

Advance organizers help students focus on key ideas by enabling them to anticipate which points are important to learn. If they are given a "mental road map" of what they have accomplished, where they are presently, and where they are going, they are more likely to understand the purpose for what they are studying and therefore set realistic goals. This strategy is particularly effective for those students who are more global learners and "see the forest before they see the individual trees." Tables of contents, overviews, focus questions, and other such devices help global learners focus. They need to understand the context to make sense of the details.

Graphic organizers are a subset of advance organizers. *Graphic organizers* are visual representations of knowledge that organize ideas and illustrate relationships. Graphic organizers exist in a variety of forms, such as webs, concept maps, story maps, flowcharts, matrixes, Venn diagrams, and cause–effect maps. They provide a way to organize information for students who take in details without knowing what is important and what is not. They have proven to be effective tools to aid learning and thinking by helping students and teachers to represent abstract information in more concrete form, portray relationships among facts and concepts, relate new information to previous experiences, and organize thoughts for problem solving.

Graphic organizers may be used before instructional activities to provide a context for integrating new information. If used during instruction, they can help students to think and reorganize information so that they can understand the relationships of the concepts and facts. If used after instruction, graphic organizers may be used to summarize learning, provide a structure for review, and serve as a means for the teacher to assess the level of student understanding.

When introducing students to a new graphic organizer, teachers should describe its purpose, model its use, and provide students with opportunities for guided practice. Once students become comfortable with using the organizer, they can apply them to a variety of situations. Teachers can then encourage students to create their own graphic organizers.

CULTURALLY CONNECTED INSTRUCTIONAL STRATEGIES

Research has suggested some culturally specific "best practices" that appear to enhance the academic success of culturally diverse groups. Some examples depicted in Figure 7 seem particularly relevant for Native American, African American, Mexican American, and Hmong students.

Call-and-Response Strategy

The call-and-response technique is an important strategy for teachers to recreate in the classroom. The purpose is to help students renew energy through

Figure 7

emotional and spiritual expression. Three elements are necessary to achieve this:

◻ A powerful vision or message is needed to activate the emotional and spiritual powers within each of us.

◻ A source—song, dance, or drums—allows for the expression of these creative powers

◻ A form of participation is needed that reinforces the power of the vision or message that in turn empowers each individual and the collective group. This form of participation synchronizes the mind and body in total engagement.

The African American cultural pattern of call and response is basic to African American expressive behavior because it forms the foundation for their collective interactions and relationships. The call-and-response strategy, a rhythmic communication form with specific response timing to drop in and drop out of the cadence, is an intense interaction between an individual and a group. The "caller" sends a message to the group ("responders") who immediately affirm the individual power and unique style of the caller. The vision and image that is being created by the caller is intensified as the responders become more actively engaged in their affirmations of the message and the caller's style. The affirmations function as the response, but also as a further signal to the caller to create an even more powerful image. This serves as an invitation to create a unifying experience to further strengthen the collective unconsciousness from which the caller and responders together draw mutual energy.

The caller can be either a teacher or a student. Traditionally, this method is used to

◻ maximize individual and group members' levels of participation;

◻ accelerate and reinforce the memory of the group through repetition and choral responsiveness;

◻ increase students' learning options from being primarily visual to being multisensory;

◻ give all students repeated opportunities to lead the group, improvise, and develop their own style in a structured, supportive situation;

◻ demonstrate culture-specific pieces for historical and aesthetic purposes.

An example was cited in the previous chapter when the Griot activity was used in the Afrocentric classroom.

Imagery–Visual Thinking Strategy

Robert McKim (1980), author of *Experiences in Visual Thinking*, defined the process as having three parts: (a) the images we see—they are images, not "things"; (b) the images we imagine in our "mind's eye"; and (c) the images we draw or paint. If teachers understand the integration of all three parts, visual thinking becomes a very powerful tool to teach Hmong and Mexican American bilingual students and to help them develop English language skills. It provides a series of natural sequences to connect their previous learning experiences to new learning. If ESL students recall an image of their past and then use their imagination to expand the image, a new enriched image is formed. If the student then draws the image, more detail is added because drawing helps to elaborate on an idea. This drawing then represents a new concept, which may be labeled with both native and English vocabulary words. This takes the student's thinking from a figural basis (the image in the mind's eye) to a symbolic basis (a drawing representing some meaning) to a semantic basis (words representing the drawing).

For example, in the scenario of the bilingual classroom, Ms. Juarez asked her students while sitting at their desks to close their eyes; put their hands on their knees palm side up; relax their legs, arms, and shoulders; and take five deep breaths. She then asked them to recall a piece of their favorite fruit from their native country. She asked them to imagine the color and the shape, to feel the texture, and to smell the aroma. She then asked them to turn the piece of fruit over in their hands, bring it close to their mouths, and take a big bite from it. With her next suggestion, the students opened their eyes and silently drew their piece of fruit. Ms. Juarez asked them to share what they had seen, felt, heard, smelled, and tasted. She listed the words that they used to describe their experience on a class experience chart so that they had an expanded list of vocabulary words to describe their fruit. Cooperative groups of three students then chose multiple new vocabulary words to develop a group story using their visuals. The students then shared them orally in a small group presentation to the rest of the class.

> When students learn in ways that are natural to them, they will experience increased academic achievement and improved self-esteem.

Visual thinking is not necessarily a linear thinking process. Students may start with an abstract drawing and use their mind's eye to imagine and construct meaning for the abstraction. On the other hand, they also might start with a word and draw their concept of the experiences they have had relative to that word. The most important thing to remember is that students use visual thinking to help them make connections and establish relationships between old and new concepts. The process of visual thinking can be learned and therefore should be taught!

Affirmations Using the Circle Strategy

A strategy used in African American and Native American traditional experiences is the affirmation of oneself relative to the collective community and universe. This practice is part of the daily routines used to explore one's roots, celebrate one's talents, promote interdependence, and build inner strength and spirituality. Affirmation relieves inner conflict, focuses actions, and integrates personal and collective values. Students generally begin and end each day with an affirmation. This helps them to focus on their responsibilities to learn to their maximum potential and reminds them of their purpose in life relative to the values of their families and communities. It also promotes their personal responsibility for the learning of others and builds a context for their actions and interactions. When selecting or developing affirmations, teachers should ensure that the classroom affirmations

> **Sample Affirmations**
> Everyday I grow smarter.
> I love doing my work.
> I am the master of my life.
> I accept myself completely.

❑ Set the tone for the day's learning

❑ Reinforce the concept that learning happens beyond the classroom

❑ Help connect the differences between the school and experiential learning in the community

❑ Respect and acknowledge that children come to school with cultural experiences from their community

❑ Reinforce the expectation that the family and their community have that all children can and will be successful academically;

❑ Include the learning environment as part of the students' real world.

This latter suggestion can be reinforced by bringing various and diverse role models into the classroom to share cultural affirmations.

The process for the affirmation strategy is as follows: Students form a circle and stand facing each other (sometimes holding hands) to recite the affirmation. The leader starts by asking everyone to be silent for 1 minute. When the group is focused, the leader begins the affirmation by reciting a phrase or a couple of lines. The followers echo the leaders. The entire group participates by reciting back exact phrases the leader uses. The leader repeats the affirmation three times using different inflections, tones, and pitches. After the third round is finished, the leader asks everyone to observe another moment of silence and directs them to envision all of their activities for the day and reflect on how the affirmation will help them individually and collectively complete their tasks successfully, and review their previous day's activities and connect what they have accomplished to what they need to do for the day. They then leave the circle and their work begins.

KIVA Process Strategy

The KIVA Process, developed by Lila N. Carol (1993), has its roots in the ancient Pueblo Native American tradition used for ceremonies and used to conduct tribal business. We have adapted this process for use in the classroom. Elements of this ancient tradition have formed the basis for a problem identification, analysis, and resolution or consensus process for students. It is important for the teacher to define the purposes of the process so that students understand that problem identification is complex and very difficult, analysis takes time, and resolution takes creativity and support from everyone. KIVA is designed so that every voice in the room is heard. Consequently, the KIVA process may take several days to complete successfully and evolves in stages. Teachers have found that KIVA can be most effective when representatives from various groups—the elders, community, family, and other mentors—interact with the teacher and students to resolve an issue.

To use the process, change the physical space so that tables and chairs are arranged in an octagon shape. The groups' representatives form concentric circles around the tables and each group is assigned to a ring. Tribal elders (or the teacher) serve as the group facilitators and stand or sit in the middle of the rings. Their role is to lead the discussion, ensure that everyone speaks, and ensure that different points of view are expressed and respected. The facilitators promote the sharing of perspectives of the representative groups and encourage looking at issues through different sets of lenses in order to promote understanding among the diverse groups.

There are several rounds of interchange in a KIVA process. A *round* is defined as the facilitators asking a series of essential questions related to the issue; each of the three representative groups respond in turn. Each ring of participants has approximately 10 minutes time to respond to the essential questions. The group sitting at the tables begins the round. After 10 minutes, that group stands up and moves to the outer ring. The other two groups move in toward the center and the second group takes its turn. This process continues until every group has had an opportunity to express itself. While the respective groups are speaking, two community members record both the questions and responses. (Another possibility is to videotape or audiotape the proceedings.) At the end of the rounds, the facilitators ask participants to prioritize what is the most important problem or best solution from the discussion. These priorities are written on color-coded cards for later analysis. The cards can be sorted according to similarities, and further explorations may be held in small group sessions where appropriate. When the KIVA reconvenes, the facilitators synthesize the similarities of viewpoints and note any significant differences. They identify any themes that have evolved, suggest possibilities for further clarification, and try to articulate the consensus of the group.

Some examples of issues that might be stimulating to address using the KIVA process include:

◻ Should all students wear uniforms? Why or why not?

◻ Should spirituality be taught in schools? Why or why not?

◻ What are student rights?

◻ Should students attend school year round? Why or why not?

Many others undoubtedly will emerge during the year.

Mnemonics—Accelerated Learning

Brain researchers claim that we only use about 4% of our brain (Ostrander & Schroeder, 1979), but the number of things we can keep in mind at any one time is limited. The average mind can recall between five and seven items. For very young children and ESL students, the limit may be one. How do we increase ESL students' memories? We need to create concrete images of sights, sounds, and feelings and to make connections between the images. Students use several strategies, depending on their developmental level of language acquisition, to make these connections and therefore increase their memory. Strategies include:

- "Chunking" groups of items so that they take up only one "space" in the working memory bank;

- Internalizing concepts so that they become automatic or subliminal rather than being a conscious effort

- Using music and rhyme as a memory aide.

Mnemonics—a learning aid used to facilitate memory— is particularly effective for students for whom English is a second language because they frequently are asked to remember large amounts of unrelated and unfamiliar information for which they have no existing memory structure. The following are the most widely used:

- *Rhyming Device*—a strategy that uses familiar rhymes to aid memory. The rhyme "Thirty days hath September . . . " is a common example of a way to remember the number of days in each month.

- *Acronym Device*—a strategy that involves creating a new word from the first letters of a series of words to be learned. The acronym ROY G BIV is a common example of a way to remember the colors on the color wheel.

- *Familiar Place Device*—a strategy that associates elements of a familiar place, such as rooms in their home, with items to be memorized.

- *Key Words Device*—a strategy that involves memorizing one or more words from a sentence to help the student remember the whole sentence. The words become a guide to the thought.

Mnemonic strategies such as those identified above can be taught to students of all ages with various learning abilities. For beginning readers, combining jingles and pictures helps create sound–symbol correspondence in key words. Teachers should vary the lesson speed according to the age and ability of the students. Students should learn to create their own mnemonic devices because the very act of creating them makes them meaningful from an experiential view.

Storytelling

As students listen to a story, a question they often ask is, "Is it real?" At a very young age, they are already able to center on one of the characteristics of a descriptive story to create a vision, whether it be reality or fantasy. According to Paul Zweig (1984), "To enter a story we must abandon ourselves. The story resembles a wind filtering through cracks in a wall: it gives evidence of the vastness. It provides a mobility through time and space like the magical mobility supplied in some old tales" (p.18). Many people consider storytelling an art form because it combines the talents of the speakers, who use their hands, bodies, and voices to express emotion, spirit, and style. Storytelling produces strong responses in both the teller and the listeners. It can be used to entertain or to educate.

In Native American tradition, the elders (wise men or women) often speak in low voices. No one interrupts another person. A sign of maturity in the children is success in their remaining silent, listening actively, and using the stories as a metaphor for application to their daily lives. Through oral tradition, children were educated and taught the wisdom and values of their people. In ancient times, the telling of stories was the key to survival. There were stories to explain all phenomena, events, mysteries, rituals, and religious traditions. Today, storytelling is still valued as a means for educating, but it also is recognized as a form of entertainment. The Sumi Indians of Nicaragua have stories for entertainment that are told in the daytime. Stories that depict lessons about life are told only at night. All tribes value storytelling because it has played a significant role in documenting the history and culture of the people, which have been passed on from generation to generation. Often that oral tradition contradicts the historical viewpoints found in textbooks.

Teaching children how to be storytellers gives them a sense of self-confidence and pride in themselves and their culture. The process of developing storytelling skills in children involves (a) encouraging them to take risks, (b) identifying individual strengths, (c) promoting a noncompetitive learning environment of sharing and respect, (d) increasing self- esteem through group support, and (e) developing critical and creative thinking skills in students.

One tool that helps develop critical and creative thinking in order to generate ideas for a story is called *attribute listing*. Students form five columns on a sheet of paper. At the top of each column, they list one of the following main categories: character, setting, time, happenings, and conflict. Under each category, they brainstorm as many possibilities as they can. To generate unique, new story lines, they randomly choose one listing from each column, which gives them a basic outline for a plot. The students generate their stories and refer to the following storytelling rubric to plan and practice their presentations of their original stories.

Connect with Oral Histories

Ask your students to interview their parents, relative, or community elders to identify a story or piece of oral history that has had great significance for their lives or that contains an important message that they would like to pass on to the next generation.

1 Set aside storytelling time each day for students to share their oral history or story.

2 Ask each student to keep a story journal that would include a page for each story told on which the students would record: Who? What? Where? When? Why?

3 Ask each student to record for each story in the journal: "What did you learn?" "How did you feel?"

Questions: What did you as the teacher learn? How did you feel? What insights did you gain about the families, traditions, and ideas of your students? Do you have a story to share with the class from your background?

The oral presentation rubric you can use to evaluate the storytelling of your students is an excellent authentic assessment device. It might look something like this:

4 = Outstanding job!
3 = Good—you're almost there
2 = Practice, practice, practice—needs more work
1 = Ask for help and practice some more

___Speaks with expressive voice
___Uses expressive gestures
___Projects voice to the audience
___Speaks clearly and is easy to understand
___Knows information in depth
___Maintains good eye contact with audience
___Uses visuals or other props
___Speaks to audience, not at it
___Demonstrates clear organization with introduction, major points, and summary
___Stays focused on main idea
___Uses creativity in style of presentation
___Uses humor

Assessment Strategy

Assessment is as much of a part of instruction as planning the activities. If done correctly, assessment determines whether learning has occurred or whether other ways of presenting the information are needed. Assessment also provides us information about the students' development and the effectiveness of the instructional activities.

Both norm-referenced and alternative assessment are needed to provide feedback on individual students and communities of students. If teachers want to be more compatible in matching students learning with instruction and assessing their progress, they must be willing to disaggregate the data on norm-referenced tests by race–ethnicity and gender. Expect to find some startling information, which, in turn, may affect your instruction!

In addition to the traditional standardized tests, there are a few norm-referenced tests that hold promise for diverse student populations. The Ravens Progressive Matrixes, certain forms of the Structure of the Intellect, and the Torrance Creativity Test provide data not usually found in other norm-referenced tests. These instruments are particularly helpful in understanding cognitive style and the preferred way of processing information.

Examining instructional and cultural style attunement is possible by using other forms that are proving to be particularly helpful in identifying competent performance. These assessment forms include the following:

❑ Objective tests which require students to make choices from lists of answers (true–false, matching, multiple choice);

- Alternative assessments, which include all other forms used to judge student learning (student projects, portfolios, essay writing, teacher interviews, teacher observations);

- Authentic assessment, which is a subset of alternative assessment that uses real-life situations as a foundation for students to make decisions (An example is performance assessment that requires students to create a product or demonstrate their knowledge in some way, as is done in storytelling and using the rubric).

In our search for best practices through action research, we find that performance assessment reflects the differences in cognitive and cultural styles because it provides opportunities for students to demonstrate their personal connections between their background experiences and their new learning. Assessment must be embedded in the curriculum to provide immediate feedback to the students so they can adjust their thinking and their approaches to the task to achieve success.

Teaching to different cultures and different learning styles is not a difficult task, but it does require the use of strategies that are more interactive, student centered, visual, and oriented toward discovery and problem solving. The techniques described in this book permit students to construct their own vision of the concepts, ideas, and events, which produces a greater involvement in the learning process. The most important component for the teacher to include is *assessment*: students must be given the opportunity to demonstrate what they have discovered and learned.

ACTION STEP VI

Plan a Change

What will you do with this information? You could use it to

- Prioritize the changes you suggested in Action Step IV.

- Identify the first five changes you will make in your classroom.

- Predict what will happen when you make the changes.

- Record what actually happened—what students said, what they did. Pay particular attention to students from different cultures than the school's. Note any similarity or difference in their reactions to your approach.

As you continue to envision and explore new horizons for yourself and your students, revisit each of the scenarios, beginning with Scenario One, Vision of the Future. Ask yourself the following questions:

1 How does this classroom reflect the belief that there are individual differences in student and teacher talents, cultural and cognitive styles, and experiences that need to be addressed in designing the climate of a more culturally compatible classroom?

2 How does this classroom reflect the belief that there are no true differences in ability on the basis of gender, culture, language, economic, or family status?

3 How does the classroom climate reflect the belief that students need to understand "self" as part of understanding differing points of view and multiple cultural perspectives?

4 How does the curriculum reflect the belief that knowledge must be actively constructed to create true understanding and meaning for students?

5 How does the classroom reflect the belief that student success is dependent on shared responsibility and collaboration among student, parent–family, school, and community?

6 How does the curriculum reflect the belief that contextual learning affects student achievement?

7 How do the activities used reflect the belief that matching instructional strategies to the cultural and cognitive style of the students is key to assuring growth in achievement of all students?

Now, look at your classroom and do the final self-audit (Exhibit 6).

EXHIBIT 6 | **Final Self-Audit of Your Culturally Compatible Classroom**

At the beginning of your journey, you completed a self audit of where you were in your developmental stage of learning how to implement a culturally compatible classroom. Now it is time to complete another self audit WHERE YOU ARE NOW IN YOUR DEVELOPMENTAL STAGE. Please rate yourself on each of the following elements using a scale of 1–5 with 5 being *making corrections/culturally responsive*, 3 is *starting to put into practice*, and 1 being *seeking understanding*.

ENVIRONMENTAL STYLE:

1. Are your visuals representative of all cultural groups?

    1   3   5

2. Do you have learning centers that capitalize and focus on the different modalities/intelligence?

    1   3   5

3. Do you establish a routine and daily schedule, to provide some important structure?

    1   3   5

4. Do you encourage interpersonal interactions and a sense of family and community?

    1   3   5

5. How would you rate your understanding and knowledge of the cultural ways of thinking, acting, and believing of the following groups:
   (1 = *low*; 3 = *average*; 5 = *high*):

    African Americans   Hmong Americans

    1   3   5   1   3   5

American Indians

☐   ☐   ☐
1   3   5

Italian American

☐   ☐   ☐
1   3   5

German Americans

☐   ☐   ☐
1   3   5

Mexican Americans

☐   ☐   ☐
1   3   5

Hispanic/Latino Americans

☐   ☐   ☐
1   3   5

INTERACTIONAL STYLE:

1. When you use cooperative groups, are you certain everyone understands their role in the performance of the task?   ☐—☐—☐   1   3   5

2. Are you prone to group heterogeneously by race, gender, and ability unless the task specifically demands another type of grouping?   ☐—☐—☐   1   3   5

3. Do you find ways to engage all students in each lesson?   ☐—☐—☐   1   3   5

4. Do you encourage formality with role definitions and appropriate etiquette?   ☐—☐—☐   1   3   5

5. Do you allow students to help each other or to work together even when reading a text?   ☐—☐—☐   1   3   5

INSTRUCTIONAL STRATEGIES FOR COGNITIVE STYLE:

1. When giving an assignment, do you provide a global view of the task as well as a step-by-step plan for what groups or individuals are to accomplish?   ☐—☐—☐   1   3   5

2. Do you operate in the classroom as a guide and facilitator rather than a "performer" in front of an audience?   ☐—☐—☐   1   3   5

3. Does "engagement" mean more to you than asking and responding to questions or worksheets?   ☐—☐—☐   1   3   5

4. Do you model and schedule opportunities to practice the ideas or concepts before you require students to demonstrate or test their understanding?   ☐—☐—☐   1   3   5

EXHIBIT 6 | CONT'D

5. If you use lectures to convey information, do you limit your presentation to 5–10 minutes and have visuals and examples as models of the concept about which you are speaking?

☐   ☐   ☐
1   3   5

6. Do you plan ways of helping students process and internalize the information that has been presented?

☐   ☐   ☐
1   3   5

7. When you use films, videos, guest speakers, or lengthy readings, do you design ways to assist students to think about and understand the information?

☐   ☐   ☐
1   3   5

INSTRUCTIONAL DESIGN FOR COGNITIVE STYLE RESPONSIVENESS:

1. Do you have each day/lesson carefully planned?

☐   ☐   ☐
1   3   5

2. Do you plan a lesson or unit with specific activities, themes, or concepts that include material or information to demonstrate connections across disciplines?

☐   ☐   ☐
1   3   5

3. Do you use the knowledge of fine arts (art, music, literature) as other ways in which students can gain knowledge about concepts or ideas?

☐   ☐   ☐
1   3   5

ASSESSMENT STYLE:

1. Do you include both qualitative and quantitative data in your assessment of: individuals? Your class? Yourself as a teacher?

☐   ☐   ☐
1   3   5

2. Have you analyzed the tests given you or the school district to ensure that the questions have an assumption of knowledge with which students are familiar or of which they will become familiar through your instruction?

☐   ☐   ☐
1   3   5

SUGGESTED READINGS

Bellanca, J., & Fogarty, R. (1991). *Blueprints for thinking in the cooperative class-room*. Palatine, IL: Skylight Publishing.

Block, C. C., & Zinke, J. (1995). *Creating a culturally enriched curriculum for grades K–6*. Boston: Allyn & Bacon.

Bruchac, J., & Caduto, M. (1991). *Native American stories*. Golden, CO: Fulcrum Publishing.

Capacchione, L. (1989). *The creative journal: The art of finding yourself*. North Hollywood, CA: Newcastle Publishing.

Cohen, E. G. (1986). *Designing groupwork*. New York: Teachers College Press.

Fletcher, A. (1994). *Indian games and dances with Native songs*. Lincoln: University of Nebraska Press.

Harmin, M. (1994). *Inspiring active learning: A handbook for teachers*. Alexandria, VA: Association of Supervision and Curriculum Development.

Kasten, W., & Clarke, B. (1993). *The multi-age classroom: A family of learners*. Katonah, NY: Richard C. Owen Publishers.

Knappert, J. (1989). *The A-Z of African proverbs*. London: Karnak House.

Lester, J. (1969). *Black folktales*. New York: Grove Weidenfeld.

Livo, N., & Cha, D. (1991). *Folk stories of the Hmong: Peoples of Laos, Thailand, and Vietnam*. Englewood, CO: Libraries Unlimited.

Shea, P. (1995). *Whispering cloth: A refugee's story*. Honesdale, PA: St. Martin's Press.

Sullivan, C. (Ed.). (1991). *Children of promise: African American literature and art for young people*. New York: Harry N. Abrams.

West, J. O. (1988). *Mexican American folklore: Legends, songs, festivals, proverbs, crafts, tales of saints, of revolutionaries, and more*. Little Rock, AK: August House Press.

final review

This book has provided you the opportunity to examine your classroom and your interaction with students who are usually perceived as deficient or are ignored totally. We hope that by using the theory and the suggestions for practice, you will create your own culturally compatible classroom that invites all students to learn.

Remember that meeting this objective requires the following:

1. Knowledge of different cultural groups;

2. The development of a warm, supportive, culturally responsive environment;

3. An awareness of different cognitive styles;

4. The inclusion of strategies that address culturally influenced styles;

5. The ability to build bridges between the students' culture and the society norms in ways that assist students to achieve without abandoning their community identity.

NOW IT IS YOUR TURN!
    When you have finished your second audit, compare your responses to both audits; then assess your growth and development.

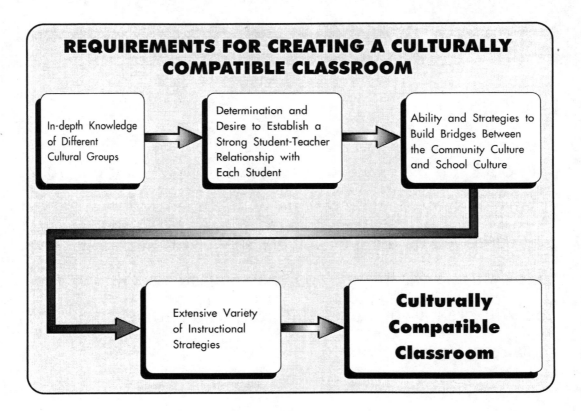

Figure 8

STOP AND REFLECT XIII | Assess Your Growth

How have you changed?
How have you stayed the same?
Which areas will you revisit for further reflection and planning?

We invite you to revisit this book as often as you can. Each time, you will discover something new and different that you can use to transform your perspective of children, their parents, their community, the profession, your classroom, and yourself.

appendix I

An Invitation to Personal Growth

Reflection becomes a very important part of professional change and growth. We invite you to keep a journal: not just an ordinary journal, but a creative journal using your "different ways of knowing" to keep a record of your journey. The purpose of this journal is twofold: to keep a record of your responses to the questions raised in the chapters and to express your personal thoughts and feelings. Use this journal to

☐ express your thoughts and feelings

☐ clarify your concerns

☐ raise your consciousness

☐ describe your ideas, choices, and decisions

☐ analyze and declare changes for implementation

☐ discover new insights related to your teaching behaviors

❑ develop new understandings of yourself and your relationship with your students.

The form of your journal should be very open-ended. Some exercises, sidebars, and reflective questions have been included to help you process and internalize the concepts being discussed. You may choose to add additional reflections that may take the form of poetry or prose, drawings, cartoons, graphs or charts, abstract designs, doodles, and other forms of mnemonic devices. By using different forms, you will discover new ways to express yourself and develop new insights.

Journaling is a very personal experience. We suggest that you find a favorite spot that is comfortable and offers you a climate of quiet reflection. Consciously reserve a specific amount of time. We suggest a minimum of 15 minutes. Use your journal when you feel like it as well as when we suggest that you "stop and reflect." It is important to complete the exercises in your journal and you also need to carry it with you so that it is there when you need it, particularly if you are trying a new strategy, a change in the way you relate to a student, or even a new seating arrangement. To use a journal for personal growth means you must be honest with yourself and sincere in your discoveries. This is a confidential tool, so ensure that your privacy is respected. Share your insights with others only if you wish. Try not to be critical of yourself and suspend your judgment. Most of all, relax, tweak your curiosity, express yourself in as many ways as you can, and enjoy!

JOURNAL REFLECTION AND DISCOVERIES

appendix II

K-W-L Chart

K-W-L Chart

What I Know	What I Want to Know	What I Learned

K-W-L Chart

What I Know	What I Want to Know	What I Learned

glossary

Attentional style—the preferred object or objects of focus.

BEV—Black English vernacular (a preferred method of speaking).

Cognitive style—the preferred way of processing information.

Cognitive style attunement—the procedures and practices that create bridges between different cognitive styles and permit simultaneous use to accomplish the same task.

Communication style—an individuals' preferred way of sending and receiving messages in a social setting. May include verbal and nonverbal methods.

Conceptual style—an individual's preferred way of categorizing information to provide meaning and purpose.

Constructivism—a process of learning through creating one's own reality.

Contextual survey—a way of assessing ideas, events, and objects in a student's environment that can be used to develop examples and projects that have a particular meaning to that student.

Cultural norms—the standards to which cultural groups adhere.

Cultural style—the pattern of attitudes, behaviors, beliefs to which individuals adhere.

Culturally compatible—a situation, event, or behavior that tolerates the harmonious existence of other cultures.

Culturally mediated—the procedures or strategies that build bridges between sets of cultural patterns or cognitive styles. Allows mutual existence of cultural patterns in the same setting.

Culture—the collective consciousness of a group of people. A set of invisible patterns that form the normal ways of acting, feeling, perceiving, judging, and organizing the world.

Expressive styles—an individual's preferred methods of facial and body gestures, movement, tone of voice, and other actions that uniquely display his or her culture or personality.

GEESA—a program available from Phi Delta Kappa designed to help teachers assess gender expectation differences as manifested in their behavior and effect on student achievement.

Information processing—the internal workings of the mind that include perceptual, conceptual, and reasoning processes.

Intuition—a way of learning or gaining knowledge through insight or cognitive leap to a discovery.

Learning style—an individual's preferred way of establishing environmental factors to facilitate study and thinking.

Linguistic style—an individual's pattern of language orientation most likely to be used by a cultural group.

Modalities—bodily senses through which an individual receives information from the environment.

Response style—an individual's preferred way of demonstrating his or her personality. Answers question "Who Am I" in relationship to events, ideas, or people.

Social interaction style—an individual's preferred way of relating to people. Tendencies usually lean toward avoiding interaction in favor of solitude or desiring interaction and being around groups of people.

TESA—Teacher Expectation and Student Achievement. A program available from Phi Delta Kappa that helps teachers identify their expectations and behaviors which might affect student achievement.

references

Arnheim, R. (1985). The double-edged mind: Intuition and the intellect. In E. Eisner (Ed.), *Learning and teaching the ways of knowing: Eighty-fourth yearbook of the National Society for the Study of Education* (Part II, pp. 77–96). Chicago: The University of Chicago Press.

Aschenbrenner, J. (1973). Extended families among Black Americans. *Journal of Comparative Family Studies, 3,* 257–268.

Au, K. H., & Jordan, C. (1978). *Creating the cross-cultural classroom: A case study.* Paper presented at the meeting of the American Anthropological Association, Los Angeles.

Banks, J. A. (1990). The dimensions of multicultural education. *Multicultural Leader, 3,* 104.

Barsch, R. H. (1971). The processing mode hierarchy as a potential deterrent to cognitive efficiency. In J. Hellmuth (Ed.), *Cognitive studies: Deficits in cognition.* New York: Bruner/Mazel.

Baugh, J. (1994). New and prevailing misconceptions of African American English for logic and mathematics. In E. R. Hollins, J. E. King, & W. C. Hayman (Eds.), *Teaching diverse populations: Formulating a knowledge base* (pp. 191–205). Albany, NY: State University of New York Press.

Baxter, J. C. (1970). Interpersonal spacing in natural settings. *Sociometry, 33,* 444–456.

Belenky, M. F., Clinchy, B. M., Goldberger, N. R., & Tarule, J. M. (1986). *Women's ways of knowing: The development of self, voice, and mind.* New York: Basic Books.

Bell, D. (1987). The world and the United States in 2013. *Daedalus, 116,* 1–31.

Bennett, C. (1979). Teaching students as they would be taught: The importance of cultural perspective. *Educational Leadership, 37,* 259–268.

Berliner, D. C., & Biddle, B. J. (1995). *The manufactured crisis: Myths, fraud and the attack on America's public schools.* Reading, MA: Addison-Wesley Publishing.

Betances, S. (1990). Understanding the dimensions of our problem. In J. G. Bain & J. L. Herman (Eds.), *Making schools work for underachieving minority students* (pp. 25–33). New York: Greenwood Press.

Birren, F. (1978). *Color and human response.* New York: Van Nostrand Reinhold.

Bloom, B. S. (1976). *Human characteristics and school learning.* New York: McGraw-Hill.

Bock, P. K. (1988). *Rethinking psychological anthropology: Continuity and change in the study of human action.* New York: W. H. Freeman.

Boring, E. G. (1930). A new ambiguous picture. *American Journal of Psychology, 42,* 444–445.

Bower, B. (1987, September 9). Asian languages and mathematics skill. *Science News, 132.*

Boykin, A. W. (1982). Task variability and the performance of Black and White school children: Vervistic explorations. *Journal of Black Studies, 12,* 469–485.

Boykin, A. W. (1994). Afrocultural expression and its implications for schooling. In E. R. Hollins, J. E. King, & W. C. Hayman, (Eds.), *Teaching diverse populations: Formulating a knowledge base* (pp. 243-256). Albany, NY: State University of New York Press.

Bradley, C., Basam, C., Axelrod, M., & Jones, E. (1990). Language and mathematics learning. *UME Trends*, pp. 7–8.

Brooks, M. (1989). *Instant rapport*. New York: Warner Books.

Brophy, J. E., & Evertson, C. (1976). *Learning from teaching: A developmental perspective*. Boston: Allyn & Bacon.

Bruner, J. S. (1960). *The process of education*. New York: Vintage Books.

Cantor, N., & Kihlstrom, J. F. (1981). *Personality, cognition and social interaction*. Hillsdale, NJ: Erlbaum.

Carol, L. N. (1993). KIVA: A leadership initiative and technique. In L. Gray (Ed.), *Leadership: Preparing leaders for changing schools* (pp. 18–20). St. Paul, MN: Minnesota Alliance of School Administrators.

Cartwright, C. (1987, August 15). Minority enrollment trends have national economic impact. *Black Issues in Higher Education, 4*, 1–2.

Clark, R. M. (1983). *Family life and school achievement*. Chicago: University of Chicago Press.

Cohen, E. G. (1986). *Designing groupwork*. New York: Teacher's College Press.

Corno, L., & Mandinach, E. B. (1983). The role of cognitive engagement in classroom learning and motivation. *Educational Psychologist, 18*, 88–108.

Cummins, J. (1992). The empowerment of Indian students. In J. Reyhner (Ed.), *Teaching American Indian students* (pp. 3–12). Norman, OK: University of Oklahoma Press.

Cummins, J., & Swain, M. (1986). *Bilingualism in education: Aspects of theory, research, and practice*. London: Longman.

Cureton, G. O. (1978). Using Black learning style. *The Reading Teacher, 41*, 751–756.

Cutrona, C. E., & Feshbach, S. (1979). Cognitive and behavioral correlates of children's differential use of social information. *Child Development, 50,* 1036–1042.

Damico, S. B. (1985). The two worlds of school differences in the photographs of Black and White adolescents. *The Urban Review, 17,* 210–222.

Dao, M. (1991). Designing assessment procedures for educationally at-risk southeast Asian-American students. *Journal of Learning Disabilities, 24*(10), 594–601; 629.

Das, J. P., Kirby, J., & Jarmon, R. F. (1975). Simultaneous and successive syntheses: An alternative model for cognitive ability. *Psychological Bulletin, 82,* 87–102.

Delgado-Gaitan, C., & Trueba, H. (1991). *Crossing cultural borders.* London: The Falmer Press.

Della Valla, J. (1984). *An experimental investigation of the word recognition scores of seventh grade students to provide supervisory and administrative guidelines for the organization of effective instructional environments.* Unpublished doctoral dissertation, St. Johns University, Jamaica, New York.

Dembo, M. H. (1988). *Applying educational psychology in the classroom* (3rd ed.). New York: Longman.

Dinges, N. C., & Hollenbeck, A. R. (1978). Field-dependence–independence in Navajo children. *International Journal of Psychology, 13,* 215–220.

DuBois, W. E. B. (1970). *The souls of Black folk.* New York: Washington Square Press. (Originally published 1903)

Dunn, R, & Dunn, K. (1975). Finding the best fit: Learning styles, teaching styles. *NAASP* Bulletin, *59,* 37–49.

Eisner, E. (1985). Aesthetic modes of knowing. In E. Eisner & K. Rehage (Eds.), *Learning and teaching: The ways of knowing: Eighty-fourth Yearbook of the National Society for the Study of Education* (Part II, pp. 23–36). Chicago: The University of Chicago Press.

Entwisle, D. R., Alexander, K. L., Pallas, A. M., & Cadigan, D. (1988). *A social psychological model of the schooling process over first grade* (Report No. HC-

1088). Baltimore: Johns Hopkins University, Center for Research on Elementary and Middle Schools.

Erickson, F. (1984). Rhetoric, anecdote and rhapsody: Coherence strategies in a conversation among Black American adolescents. In Tannen, D. (Ed.), *Coherence in spoken and written discourse*. Norwood, MJ: Ablex.

Farr, M. (1986). Language, culture and writing: Sociolinguistic foundations of research on writing. In E. Z. Rothkopf (Ed.), *Review of Research in Education Vol. 13* (pp. 195–223). Washington, DC: American Educational Research Association.

Feldman, R. S. (1985). Nonverbal behavior, race, and the classroom teacher. *Theory Into Practice, 24*, 45–49.

Fordham, S. (1988). Racelessness as a factor in Black students' school success: Pragmatic strategy or pyrrhic victory. *Harvard Educational Review, 58*, 54–84.

Fordham, S., & Ogbu, J. U. (1986). Black students' school success: Coping with the "burden of 'acting white.' " *The Urban Review, 18*, 176–206.

Frederiksen, N., Carlson, S., & Ward, W. C. (1984). The place of social intelligence in a taxonomy of cognitive abilities. *Intelligence, 8*, 315–337.

Garcia, E. E. (1991). Bilingualism, second language acquisition, and the education of Chicano language minority students. In R. R. Valencia (Ed.), *Chicano school failure and success: Research and policy agendas for the 1990s* (pp. 93–118). New York: The Falmer Press.

Gardner, H. (1983). *Frames of mind: The theory of multiple intelligences*. New York: Basic Books.

Good, T. L., & Brophy, J. E. (1977). *Educational psychology: A realistic approach*. New York: Holt, Rinehart & Winston.

Goody, J. (1977). *The domestication of the savage mind*. Cambridge, England: Cambridge University Press.

Grossman, H. (1984). *Educating Hispanic students: Cultural implications for instruction, classroom management, counseling, and assessment*. Springfield, IL: Charles C. Thomas Publishers.

Grossman, H. (1991). Special education in a diverse society: Improving services for minority and working-class students. *Preventing School Failure, 36*(1), 19–27.

Hale, J. E. (1982). *Black children: Their roots, culture, and learning styles.* Provo, UT: Brigham Young University.

Hall, E. T. (1989). Unstated features of the cultural context of learning. *Educational Forum, 54,* 21–34.

Hallpike, C. R. (1979). *The foundations of primitive thought.* Oxford, England: Clarendon.

Hamill, J. F. (1990). *Ethno-logic: The anthropology of human reasoning.* Urbana, Ill: The University of Illinois Press.

Heath, S. B. (1983). *Ways with words.* New York: Cambridge University Press.

Heck, S. F. (1978). The creative classroom environment: A stage-set design. *Journal of Creative Behavior, 12,* 120–133.

Henderson, D. H., & Washington, A. G. (1975). Cultural differences and the education of Black children: An alternative model for program development. *Journal of Negro Education, 44,* 353–360.

Hernandez, J. S. (1993). Bilingual metacognitive development. *The Educational Forum, 54*(4), 350–358.

Herskovits, M. J. (1939). The ancestry of the American Negro. *American Scholar, 8,* 84–94

Hilliard, A. G., III. (1976). *Alternatives to IQ testing: An approach to the identification of gifted minority children.* San Francisco, CA: San Francisco State University.

Hilliard, A. G., III (1989). Teachers and Cultural Styles in a Pluralistic Society. *National Education Association Journal,* 65–69.

Hollins, E. R. (1996). *Culture in school learning: Revealing the deep meaning.* Mahwah, NJ: Erlbaum.

Hood-Smith, N. E., & Leffingwell, R. J. (1983). The impact of physical space alteration on disruptive classroom behavior: A case study. *Education, 104,* 224–230.

Hsu, F. L. K. (1983). *Rugged individualism reconsidered.* Knoxville: University of Tennessee Press.

Igoa, C. (1995). *The inner world of the immigrant child.* New York: St. Martin's Press.

Johnson, D. W., & Johnson, R. T. (1994). Cooperative learning in the culturally diverse classroom. In R. A. DeVillar, C. J. Faltis, & J. P. Cummins, (Eds.), *Cultural diversity in schools: From rhetoric to practice* (pp. 57–73). Albany: State University of New York Press.

Jordan, C., & Tharp, R. G. (1979). Culture and education. In A. J. Marsella, R. G. Tharp, & T. J. Ciborowski (Eds.), *Perspectives on cross-cultural psychology* (pp. 265–285). San Diego, CA: Academic Press.

Jung, C. J. (1959). *Psychological types.* London: Routledge & K. Paul.

Kagan, S., & Zahn, L. (1975). Field dependence and school achievement gap between Anglo-American and Mexican American children. *Journal of Educational Psychology, 67,* 643–650.

Kaulback, B. (1984). Styles of learning among Native children: A review of the research. *Canadian Journal of Native Education, 11,* 27–37.

Keil, C. (1966). *Urban blues.* Chicago: University of Chicago Press.

King, J. E. (1994). The purpose of schooling for African American children: Including cultural knowledge. In E. R. Hollins, J. E. King, & W. C. Hayman (Eds.), *Teaching diverse populations: Formulating a knowledge base* (pp. 25–56). Albany, NY: State University of New York Press.

Kochman, T. (1981). *Black and White: Styles in conflict.* Chicago: The University of Chicago Press.

Kohl, H. (1988). *Thirty-six children.* New York: Plume/Penguin Books. (Original work published 1967)

Labov, W. (1972). *Language in the inner city*. Philadelphia: University of Pennsylvania Press.

Ladson-Billings, G. (1990). Culturally relevant teaching. *College Board Review*, *155*, 20–25.

Ladson-Billings, G. (1994). *The dreamkeepers*. San Francisco: Jossey-Bass Publishers.

Leap, W. L. (1992). American Indian English. In J. Reyhner (Ed.), *Teaching American Indian students* (pp. 143–153). Norman, OK: University of Oklahoma Press.

Lein, L. (1973). Black American migrant children: Their speech at home and school. *Anthropology and Education Quarterly*, *6*, 1–11.

LeVine, R. A. (1991). Discussion. In P. M. Greenfield & R. R. Cocking (Chairs), *Continuities and discontinuitites in the cognitive socialization of minority children*. Proceedings of a workshop, Department of Health and Human Services, Public Health Service, Alcohol, Drug Abuse and Mental Health Administration, Washington, DC.

Levinson, A. (1992, September 6). Barring Blacks from mainstream costs billions. *The Racine Journal Times*.

Levy, G. (1990). *Ghetto school*. Indianapolis, IN: Bobbs-Merrill, Inc. (Original work published in 1970)

Levy, N., Murphy C., & Carlson, R. (1972). Personality types among Negro college students. *Educational and Psychological Measurements*, *32*, 641–653.

Little Soldier, L. (1992). Building optimum learning environments for Navajo students. *Childhood Education*, *68*, 145–148.

Locke, D. C. (1992). *Increasing multicultural understanding*. Newbury Park, CA: Sage Publications.

Losey, K. M. (1995). Mexican American students and classroom interaction: An overview and critique. *Review of Educational Research*, *65*, 283–318.

Maehr, M. L. (1974). *Sociocultural origins of achievement*. Monterey, CA: Brooks/Cole Publishing.

Martin, E. & Martin, J. M. (1978). *The Black extended family*. Chicago: University of Chicago Press, 1978.

Martinez, J. L. (1977). *Chicano psychology*. New York: Academic Press.

McClelland, D. C. (1960). *The achieving society*. Princeton, NJ: Van Nostrand.

McKim, R. (1980). *Experiences in visual thinking*. Boston: PWF Publications.

Mehrabian, A. (1976). *Public places and private spaces*. New York: Basic Books.

Messick, S. (1994). The matter of style: Manifestations of personality in cognition, learning, and teaching. *Educational Psychologist, 29*(3), 121–136.

Miner, H. (1956). Body ritual among the Nacirema. *American Anthropologist, 58*(3), 503–507.

Moody, C. (1990). Teacher effectiveness. In J. G. Bain & J. E. Herman (Eds.), *Making schools work for underachieving minority students* (pp. 159–163). New York: Greenwood Press.

Moos, R. H. (1979). *Evaluating educational environments*. San Francisco: Jossey-Bass.

More, A. J. (1987). Indian students and their learning styles: Research results and classroom applications. *British Columbia Journal of Special Education, 11*, 23–37.

Morgan, H. (1990). Assessment of students' behavioral interactions during on-task classroom activities. *Perceptual and Motor Skills, 70*, 563–569.

Moses, R., Kamii, M., Swap, S., & Howard, J. (1989). The Algebra Project: Organizing in the spirit of Ella. *Harvard Educational Review, 59*, 413–443.

Myers, I. B. (1980). *Gifts' differing*. Palo Alto, CA: Consulting Psychologists Press.

Narisetti, R. (1995, September 8). Manufacturers decry a shortage of workers while rejecting many. *Wall Street Journal*, p. 1.

Nel, J., & Seckinger, D. S. (1993). Johann Heinrich Pestalozzi in the 1990's: Implications for today's multicultural classrooms. *The Educational Forum, 57*, 394–401.

Nobles, W. W. (1990, January). *Infusion of African and African American culture*. Keynote address at the annual conference, Academic and Cultural Excellence: An Investment in our future, Detroit Public Schools, Detroit, MI.

Noddings, N., & Shore, P. J. (1984). *Awakening the inner eye: Intuition in education*. New York: Teachers College Press.

North, M. (1978). *Personality assessment through movement*. Boston, MA: Plays, Inc.

Ogbu, J. U. (1992). Understanding cultural diversity and learning. *Educational Researcher, 21*, 5–13.

Orr, E. W. (1987). *Twice as less: Black English and the performance of Black students in mathematics and science*. New York: Norton.

Ostrander, S., & Schroeder, L. (1979). *Super-learning*. New York: Dell.

Palincsar, A. S., & Brown, A. L. (1986). Interactive teaching to promote independent learning from text. *The Reading Teacher, 39*, 771–777.

Pasteur, A. B., & Toldson, I. L. (1982). *Roots of soul: The psychology of Black expressiveness*. Garden City, NY: Anchor Press/Doubleday.

Pepper, F. C., & Henry, S. L. (1986). Social and cultural effects on Indian learning style: Classroom implications. *Canadian Journal of Native Education, 13*, 54–61.

Perkins, E. (1975). *Home is a dirty street: The social oppression of Black children*. Chicago: Third World Press.

Philips, S. U. (1983). *The invisible culture: Communication in classroom and community on the Warm Springs Indian reservation*. New York: Longman.

Polanyi, M. (1966). *The tacit dimension*. New York: Doubleday & Company.

Prichard, A., & Taylor, J. (1978). Suggestopedia for the disadvantaged reader. *Academic Therapy, 14*, 81–90.

Probst, R. (1974). Human needs and working places. *School Review, 82*, 617–620.

Purkey, W. W., & Novak, J. M. (1984). *Inviting school success. A self-concept approach to teaching and learning.* Belmont, CA: Wadsworth Publishing Company.

Ramirez, M., & Castaneda, A. (1974). *Cultural democracy, bicognitive development, and education.* San Diego, CA: Academic Press.

Reyhner, J. (Ed.). (1992). *Teaching American Indian students.* Norman, OK: University of Oklahoma Press.

Ruble, D. N., & Nakamura, C. Y. (1972). Task versus social orientation in young children and their attention to relevant social cues. *Child Development, 43,* 471–480.

Rychlak, J. F. (1975). Affective assessment, intelligence, social class and racial learning style. *Journal of Personality and Social Psychology, 32,* 989–995.

Schmeck, R. R., & Meier, S. T. (1984). Self-reference as a learning strategy and a learning style. *Human Learning, 3,* 9–17.

Shade, B. J. (1978). Sociopsychological characteristics of achieving Black children. *Negro Educational Review, 29,* 80–86.

Shade, B. J. (1982). Afro-American cognitive style: A variable in school success. *Review of Educational Research, 52,* 219–244.

Shade, B. J. (1989a). The culture and style of Mexican–American society. In B. J. Shade (Ed.), *Culture, Style, and the educative process* (pp. 43–48). Springfield, IL: Charles C Thomas.

Shade, B. J. (1989b). *Culture, style and the educative process.* Springfield, IL: Charles C Thomas Publishers.

Shade, B. J. (1989c). The influence of perceptual development on cognitive style: Cross-ethnic comparisons. *Early Child Development and Care, 51,* 137–155.

Shade, B. J. (1994). Understanding the African American learner. In E. R. Hollins, J. E. King, & W. C. Hayman. *Teaching diverse populations: Formulating a new knowledge base* (pp. 175–189). Albany, NY: State University of New York Press.

Shils, E. (1967). Color, the universal intellectual community and the Afro-Asian intellectual. *Daedleus: Color and Race*, *96*, 270–286.

Sizemore, B. (1990). Effective education for underachieving African-Americans. In J. G. Bain & J. L. Herman (Eds.), *Making schools work for underachieving minority students* (pp. 39–52). New York: Greenwood Press.

Smith, M. (1996). *Contemporary Indian cultural values*. Unpublished manuscript. Oshkosh, WI: University of Wisconsin-Oshkosh.

Smith, R. R., & Lewis, R. (1985). Race as a self-schema affecting recall in Black children. *Journal of Black Psychology*, *12*, 15–29.

Smith, V., Brown, R., & Foley, N. (1993, September). *Who are Asian Americans?* Paper presented for the Experimental Certification Program, University of Wisconsin-Parkside, Kenosha, WI.

Smitherman, G. (1991). Talkin and testifyin: Black English and the Black experience. In R. Jones (Ed.), *Black psychology* (pp. 249–264). Berkeley, CA: Cobb & Henry.

Sowell, T. (1976). Patterns of Black excellence. *The Public Interest*, *37*, 26–58.

St. John, N. (1971). Thirty-six teachers: Their characteristics and outcomes for Black and White pupils. *American Educational Research Journal*, *8*, 634–648.

Stack, C. B. (1974). *All our kin: Strategies for survival in a Black community*. New York: Harper & Row.

Stigler, J. W., & Baranes, R. (1988). Culture and mathematics learning. In E. Z. Rothkopf (Ed.), *Review of Research in Education* (Vol. 15, pp. 253–306). Washington, DC: American Educational Research Association.

Suina, J. H., & Smolkin, L. B. (1994). From natal culture to school culture to dominant society culture: Supporting transitions for Pueblo Indian students. In P. M. Greenfield & R. R. Cocking (Eds.), *Cross-cultural roots of minority child development* (pp. 115–130). Hillsdale, NJ: Erlbaum.

Sutro, E., & Gross, R. E. (1984). The five senses in teaching. *Education Digest*, *50*, 52–55.

Swift, M. S., & Spivak, G. (1973). Academic success and classroom behavior in secondary schools. *Exceptional Children, 39,* 392–399.

Swisher, K., & Deyhle, D. (1992). Adapting instruction to culture. In J. Reyhner (Ed.), *Teaching American Indian students* (pp. 81–95). Norman, OK: University of Oklahoma Press.

Sylwester, R. (1995). *A celebration of neurons: An educator's guide to the human brain.* Alexandria, VA: Association for Supervision and Curriculum Development.

Tharp, R. G. (1989). Psychocultural variables and constants: Effects on teaching and learning in schools. *American Psychologist, 44*(2), 349–359.

Tharp, R. G. (1994). Intergroup differences among Native Americans in socialization and child cognition: An ethnogenetic analysis. In P. M. Greenfield & R. R. Cocking (Eds.), *Cross-cultural roots of minority child development* (pp. 87–105). Hillsdale, NJ: Erlbaum.

Timm, J. T. (1994). Hmong values and American education. *Equity and Excellence in Education, 27*(2), 36–44.

Timm, J. T., & Chiang, B. (1997). The impact of culture on Hmong students' learning and cognitive style. In B. J. Shade (Ed.), *Culture, style, and the educative process* (2nd Ed.). Springfield, IL: Charles C. Thomas.

Triandis, H. C. (1990). Cross-cultural studies of individualism and collectivism. In J. J. Berman (Ed.), *Cross-Cultural Perspectives. Nebraska Symposium on Motivation* (pp. 41–133). Lincoln, NE: University of Nebraska Press.

Trueba, H. T. (1988). English literacy acquisition: From cultural trauma to learning disabilities in minority students. *Linguistics and Education, 1,* 125–152.

Trueba, H. T., Jacobs, L., & Kirton, E. (1990). *Cultural conflict and adaptation: The case of Hmong children in American Society.* New York: The Falmer Press.

Usdansky, M. (1992, May 29). Immigrant tide surges in 80's: USA's decade of change. *USA Today,* p. 1.

Utley, C. A. (1983). *A cross-cultural investigation of field-independence/field dependence as a psychological variable in Menominees Native American and Euro-American grade school children.* Unpublished manuscript, Wisconsin Center for Education and Research, Madison, WI.

Valencia, R. R. (Ed.). (1991). *Chicano school failure and success: Research and policy agendas for the 1990s.* London: The Falmer Press.

Vander Zanden, J. W., & Pace, A. (1984). *Educational Psychology in Theory and Practice.* New York: Random House.

Vansertima, I. (1971). African linguistic and mythological structures in the new world. In R. L. Goldstein (Ed.), *Black life and culture in the United States* (pp. 12–35). New York: Thomas Y. Crowell.

Veldman, D. J., & Worsham, M. (1982). Types of student classroom behavior. *Journal of Educational Research, 76,* 204–209.

Webster, S. T. (1974). *The education of Black Americans.* New York: Intext Educational Publishers.

Weinberg, M. (1977). *A chance to learn: The history of race and education in the United States.* Cambridge, MA: Cambridge University Press.

Williams, J. D., & Snipper, G. C. (1990). *Literacy and bilingualism.* New York: Longman Press.

Willis, F. N. (1966). Initial speaking distance as a function of the speakers' relationship. *Psychoanalytic Science, 5,* 221–222.

Willis, M. G. (1989). Learning styles of African American children: A review of the literature and interventions. *The Journal of Black Psychology, 16*(1), 47–65.

Witkin, H. A. (1978). *Cognitive styles in personal and cultural adaptation.* Hartford, CT: Clark University Press.

Witkin, H. A., Moore, C. S., Goodenough, D. R., & Cox, P. W. (1977). Field dependent and field-independent cognitive styles and their educational implications. *Review of Educational Research, 47,* 1–64.

Zweig, P. (1984). The adventure of storytelling. *The National Storytelling Journal, 1*(4), 18–22.

additional resources

Gay, G., & Baber, W. (Eds.). (1987). *Expressively Black: The cultural basis of ethnic identity*. New York: Praeger.

Goldstein, K., & Scherer, M. (1941). Abstract and concrete behaviors: An experimental study with special tests. *Psychological Monographs, 53*. (No. 239.)

Halverson, B. (1976). *Cognitive style of preschool Seminole Indian children*. Unpublished doctoral dissertation, Florida State University, Tallahassee.

Harris, P. R., & Moran, R. T. (1979). *Managing cultural differences*. Houston, TX: Gulf Publishing Company.

Kitano, M. K., & Chin, P. C. (Eds.). (1986). *Exceptional Asian children and youth*. Reston, VA: Council for Exceptional Children.

Nisbet, J., & Shucksmith, J. (1986). *Learning strategies*. London: Routledge & Kegan Paul.

Rogoff, B., & Chavajay, P. (1995). What's become of research on the cultural basis of cognitive development? *American Psychologist, 50*(10), 859–877.

Shade, B. J. (1983). *Afro-American patterns of cognition.* Unpublished manuscript, Wisconsin Center for Education Research, Madison, WI.

Silverstein, B., & Krate, R. (1975). *Children of the dark ghetto: A developmental psychology.* New York: Praeger.

Tidwell, B. J. (Ed.). (1994). *The state of Black America in 1994.* New York: National Urban League.

ABOUT THE AUTHORS

Barbara J. Shade, PhD, is a professor of educational psychology in the Department of Teacher Education at the University of Wisconsin—Parkside, where she previously served as the Dean of the School of Education. She taught in Milwaukee Public Schools, was the director of the Dane County Head Start program in Madison, Wisconsin, and worked as an urban education consultant for the Wisconsin Department of Public Instruction. In addition to providing numerous workshops to urban school faculty throughout the country, she is the author of *Culture, Style, and the Educative Process: Making Schools Work for Racially Diverse Students* (1989, 1997, Charles C. Thomas) and has published extensively in the area of cultural influences on education.

Cynthia Kelly is the Multicultural Education Coordinator for Minneapolis Public schools. She is a member of the National Association of Female Executives, National Association for Multicultural Education, and the State and National Alliance of Black School Educators. She has worked as the Equal Educational Opportunity Specialist for the Minnesota Department of Education and as a consultant to the St. Cloud University Special Education Department.

Mary Oberg is the K–12 Science Coordinator and Instructional Strategies Coordinator for Special District #1 of Minnesota Public Schools. She is an adjunct faculty member at the University of St. Thomas, the University of Minnesota, the University of Wisconsin—River Falls, Saint Mary's University of Minnesota, and Hamline University. She is a member of the Association for Supervision of Curriculum Development and the Council for Exceptional Children.